Goose berry Patch Co.

A Country Store In Your Mailbox®

W9-CBD-631

From Grandma's Kitchen

A Country Store In Your Mailbox®

Gooseberry Patch
600 London Road
Department Book
Delaware, OH 43015

★

1·800·854·6673
gooseberrypatch.com

Copyright 2002, Gooseberry Patch 1-931890-17-X
Second Printing, January, 2003

How To Subscribe

Would you like to receive
"A Country Store in Your Mailbox"®?
For a 2-year subscription to our 96-page
Gooseberry Patch catalog, simply send $3.00 to:

Gooseberry Patch ★ P.O. Box 190 ★ 600 London Road ★ Delaware, Ohio 43015

Contents

Dedication

DEDICATED TO GRANDMAs EVERYWHERE...
FOR YOUR SWEET SMILES, WARM HUGS
& YUMMY FOOD SERVED WITH LOVE!

Appreciation

FOR OUR FRIENDS WHO SHARED a
FAVORITE RECIPE. <u>THANKS</u>... YOU WARM
OUR HEARTS!

HOME-STYLE
break-fasts

Breakfast Delights

Marlene Lambie
Camdenton, MO

Whenever I serve this to my family, they always ask for seconds...especially the grandchildren!

2 8-oz. pkgs. cream cheese,
   softened
2 c. sugar, divided
1 egg yolk
1 t. vanilla extract

24-oz. loaf sliced white bread,
   crusts trimmed
cinnamon to taste
1 c. butter, melted

Mix together cream cheese, 1/2 cup sugar, egg yolk and vanilla. Spread one tablespoon mixture on each slice of bread. Roll slice from one corner to the other. Mix cinnamon and remaining sugar together in a shallow bowl. Dip rolled bread in melted butter, then roll in cinnamon-sugar mixture. Place rolls on ungreased baking sheets. Freeze rolls at least 20 minutes. Bake at 350 degrees for 8 to 10 minutes until hot and bubbly. Makes about 2 dozen.

Weekend sleepyheads love to wake up to the aroma of breakfast in the air. So, before they come downstairs, make the table look extra-special...daisies tucked in glass milk bottles and a colorful tablecloth made from vintage-style oilcloth really add fun.

Come-On-Over Crumb Cake

Elizabeth Andrus
Gooseberry Patch

After my grandmother sent her children and husband on their way in the morning, a quick call to a favorite neighbor was in order to share crumb cake and a cup of coffee before beginning the day's housework.

2 T. oil
1 egg
1/2 c. milk
2 t. vanilla extract
1/2 c. sugar

1-1/2 c. all-purpose flour
2-1/2 t. baking powder
1/2 t. salt
Garnish: powdered sugar

In a large mixing bowl, combine all ingredients. Pour in an ungreased 12"x8" baking pan, spreading to edges with spatula. Sprinkle topping over batter. Bake at 325 degrees for 30 minutes, rotating pan after 15 minutes. Remove, cool and dust with powdered sugar. Cut into squares. Serves 6.

Topping:

2-1/2 c. all-purpose flour
1 c. brown sugar, packed

2-1/2 t. cinnamon
1 c. butter, melted and cooled

Combine flour, sugar and cinnamon in a large mixing bowl. Pour butter over top; mix with hands until large crumbs form.

Ham & Cheddar Baked Eggs

Mary Scurti
Highland, CA

Green chilies give this old-fashioned favorite a new taste. It could even be garnished with sour cream and salsa if you'd like.

6 slices bread
2 c. cooked ham, diced
2 c. shredded Cheddar cheese
4-1/2 oz. can chopped green
   chilies

1 t. dry mustard
3 c. milk
8 eggs, beaten
1 t. salt

Spray a 13"x9" baking pan with non-stick vegetable spray; line the bottom with bread slices. Layer ham, cheese and chilies on top; sprinkle mustard over top. Combine milk, eggs and salt; pour over mixture. Cover and refrigerate overnight. Bake, uncovered, at 350 degrees for one hour or until center tests done. Serves 6 to 8.

Feeding a crowd? Keep pancakes, waffles, toast or biscuits warm by placing them in a single layer on a wire rack or baking sheet in a 200-degree oven.

Cheddar-Apple Biscuits

Tammie Jones
Lincolnton, NC

*Apples and cheese taste great together...especially when
paired with brown sugar and cinnamon.*

1/3 c. brown sugar, packed
2 T. all-purpose flour
1/2 t. cinnamon
10-oz. tube refrigerated
   buttermilk biscuits

1 c. shredded Cheddar cheese
2 apples, cored, peeled
   and sliced into rings
1 T. butter, melted

Combine first 3 ingredients in a small bowl; set aside. Press each
biscuit into a 3-inch circle. Place on lightly greased baking sheets;
sprinkle each with cheese and top with an apple ring. Sprinkle with
sugar mixture and drizzle with melted butter. Bake at 350 degrees for
15 minutes or until crust is golden. Makes 10 servings.

*Cookie cutters make breakfast a treat...use them
to cut out biscuit dough, shape pancakes or
cut shapes from the centers of French toast. Use
mini cutters to make the sweetest pats of butter!*

Grandma's Old-Fashioned Doughnuts

Cheri Emery
Quincy, IL

Easier to make than you'd think, and so delicious!

4 c. all-purpose flour
4 t. baking powder
1/2 t. salt
1 c. sugar
1 c. cinnamon
2 eggs, beaten

1 c. milk
2 T. margarine, softened
1 t. vanilla extract
oil for deep frying
Garnish: sugar

Sift together dry ingredients; set aside. In a separate bowl, combine all remaining ingredients except oil; gradually add dry ingredients until well mixed. Turn dough out onto a floured surface; roll to 1/2-inch thickness. Cut dough with a doughnut or biscuit cutter or the top of a 3-inch diameter glass dipped in sugar. Fry in 360-degree oil until golden. Roll in sugar while still warm. Makes about 2 dozen.

Make oh-so-simple maple butter as a tasty change for topping waffles, pancakes or biscuits...just whip 1/2 cup butter with one cup of maple syrup.

Blueberry Breakfast Cake

Linda Brostad
Minneapolis, MN

Bursting with blueberries, this is a great make-ahead recipe when family & friends are coming to visit.

2 c. blueberries
1-1/2 c. plus 2 T. all-purpose
  flour, divided
1 t. baking powder
1/2 t. salt
1/2 c. butter

1 c. sugar
2 eggs
1/3 c. milk
1 t. vanilla extract
Garnish: sugar

Toss blueberries in 2 tablespoons flour; set aside. Sift together remaining flour, baking powder and salt; set aside. Cream butter and sugar together until light and fluffy; add eggs, one at a time, beating well. Add flour mixture to creamed mixture alternately with milk. Mix for 5 minutes. Stir in vanilla and floured blueberries. Pour into a well-greased 8"x8" baking pan. Sprinkle top with sugar. Bake at 350 degrees for 35 to 40 minutes. Serves 6 to 8.

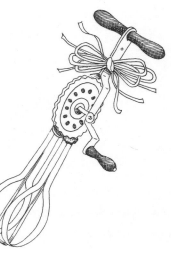

Let everyone choose their favorite juice for breakfast. Fill old-fashioned glass milk bottles with a variety of juices, and then tuck them in a wire milk bottle carrier...so easy to pass around the table!

Chocolate Chip Pancakes

Carolyn Demel
Houston, TX

*These ooey-gooey pancakes don't need syrup, but you'll want
to make sure there are plenty of napkins on hand!*

1 c. milk
2 eggs, beaten
2 c. buttermilk biscuit
   baking mix

1/4 t. cinnamon
1/2 c. mini semi-sweet
   chocolate chips
Optional: powdered sugar

Combine first 4 ingredients, stirring until moistened. Fold in chocolate
chips, being sure not to over-blend. Drop by 1/4 cupfuls onto a hot,
greased griddle; flip over when bubbles appear around edges. Cook on
each side until lightly golden. Sprinkle with powdered sugar, if desired.
Makes 12 to 16 pancakes.

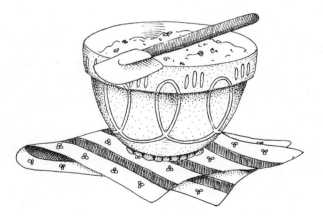

*Did you know you can use mashed bananas for all
or part of the liquid in pancake recipes? The end
result is extra-moist pancakes loaded with flavor.*

Pumpkin Waffles

Kristina Wyatt
Madera, CA

*I love to serve these topped with butter, maple syrup
and a sprinkling of toasted pecans.*

2-1/4 c. all-purpose flour
1/4 c. brown sugar, packed
4 t. baking powder
1-1/2 t. cinnamon
1 t. nutmeg
1/4 t. ground cloves

1/2 t. ground ginger
4 eggs, separated
2 c. milk
1 c. canned pumpkin
1/4 c. butter, melted

Combine first 7 ingredients in a large bowl; set aside. In a separate
bowl, mix together egg yolks, milk and pumpkin; add to flour mixture,
stirring until just moistened. Stir in butter; set aside. Beat egg whites at
high speed until soft peaks form; fold into waffle batter. Heat oiled
waffle iron according to manufacturer's directions. Depending on size
of waffle iron, pour 1/2 cup to 1-1/2 cups batter onto hot iron. Bake
for 4 to 5 minutes or until steaming stops. Repeat with remaining
batter. Makes 12 to 16 waffles.

*Extra waffles can be popped in the freezer and
reheated in a toaster for a fast weekday breakfast!*

Country Biscuits & Eggs

Kelly Brauer
Rogers, AR

Buttermilk biscuits topped with cheesy eggs and bacon...one taste and you'll know why it's a hit!

7-1/2 oz. tube refrigerated
    buttermilk biscuits
6 eggs, beaten
1/3 c. milk
salt and pepper to taste

2 T. butter
3-oz. pkg. cream cheese,
    softened and cubed
6 slices bacon, crisply cooked
    and crumbled

Press biscuits onto bottom and up sides of a 9" round pan to form crust; bake as directed. Combine eggs, milk, salt and pepper in a mixing bowl. Melt butter in a medium skillet over low heat; add egg mixture. Cook slowly, stirring occasionally, until eggs begin to set. Add cream cheese, stirring until cheese melts and eggs set completely. Spoon eggs into biscuit crust and top with bacon. Slice into wedges. Serves 6.

Mom will love breakfast in bed when it's served on a tray filled with special memories. Remove the glass from a serving tray and slide in a piece of cardstock that's the same size. Layer on a collage of favorite things...photos, ticket stubs, kids' art or pressed flowers, then gently replace the glass top.

Overnight Egg & Sausage Bake

Judy Schroeder
Sedgwick, KS

Breakfast favorites are all combined in this simple, make-ahead casserole.

1 lb. ground sausage, browned
9 eggs, beaten
3 c. milk
1/4 c. onion, chopped
1/4 c. green pepper, chopped
1 t. salt

pepper to taste
3 slices bread, cubed
1 c. shredded sharp
   Cheddar cheese
1/2 c. shredded Swiss cheese

Mix together all ingredients; pour into a well greased 13"x9" baking pan. Cover and refrigerate overnight. Bake at 350 degrees for 45 minutes. Serves 8.

The first day of school usually means a busy morning, so why not make a simple overnight breakfast casserole? Putting it together the night before means less fuss in the morning and the kids get a great start to the day!

Melt-In-Your-Mouth Biscuits

*Sherri Hagel
Spokane, WA*

*Split and served with butter and jam or topped with sausage gravy,
these flaky biscuits live up to their name.*

1-1/2 c. all-purpose flour
1/2 c. whole-wheat flour
4 t. baking powder
1/2 t. salt
2 T. sugar

1/4 c. chilled butter
1/4 c. shortening
2/3 c. milk
1 egg, beaten

Sift flours, baking powder, salt and sugar together; cut in butter and
shortening. Add milk; stir in egg. Knead on a floured surface; roll out
to 1/2-inch thickness. Cut with a biscuit cutter; place biscuits on
ungreased baking sheets. Bake at 450 degrees for 10 to 15 minutes.
Makes one to 2 dozen.

Sausage Gravy

*Leslie Stimel
Gooseberry Patch*

It's a snap to make this delicious, homestyle gravy.

1 lb. ground sausage
1/4 c. all-purpose flour
3 to 4 c. milk

1/2 t. salt
1/4 t. pepper

Heat sausage in a large skillet over medium-high heat until browned,
about 10 minutes. Stir in flour until mixture becomes thick. Reduce
heat to medium-low and gradually add milk, stirring constantly, until
mixture is thick and bubbly. Add salt and pepper. Serves 4 to 6.

Grandpa's Fried Potatoes

Michele Olds
Avon Lake, OH

*Alongside eggs, any style, these potatoes make a
great breakfast even better.*

3 to 4 lbs. potatoes
1 lb. bacon
1 onion, chopped

seasoned salt to taste
salad seasoning to taste

Boil potatoes until tender; allow to cool, then peel and cube. Fry bacon
and onion together in a large skillet; add potatoes and seasonings.
Cook until golden. Serves 6 to 8.

Sugar Plum Bacon

Karen Pilcher
Burleson, TX

Bacon with a sweet brown sugar and cinnamon coating.

1/2 c. brown sugar, packed
1 t. cinnamon

8 slices bacon, cut in half
   crosswise

Combine sugar and cinnamon in a small bowl. Dip each bacon piece in
sugar mixture to coat. Twist each piece and place on a broiler pan
lined with aluminum foil. Bake at 350 degrees for 15 to 20 minutes
until bacon is crisp and sugar is bubbly. Place bacon on aluminum foil
to cool. Makes 16 pieces.

*Why wait? Start a family reunion bright & early
with a hearty breakfast gathering! A big handmade
sign posted in the yard is sure to welcome everyone.*

Sour Cream Coffee Cake

Gloria Kaufmann
Orrville, OH

My daughter had a morning wedding and chose this as her wedding cake...it's delicious!

1 c. margarine	2 t. baking powder
1 c. sugar	1 t. baking soda
3 eggs	1/8 t. salt
1 c. sour cream	1 t. vanilla extract
2-1/2 c. all-purpose flour	1 t. lemon extract

Cream margarine and sugar thoroughly. Add eggs, one at a time, beating well after each addition. Gradually mix in sour cream. Combine dry ingredients in a separate bowl, then add to creamed mixture. Add vanilla and lemon extract. Spread batter, one-inch thick, into 2 greased 8" round baking pans. Sprinkle with 2/3 streusel topping. Pour remaining batter into pans and sprinkle with remaining streusel topping. Bake at 375 degrees for 30 minutes. Makes 12 to 16 servings.

Streusel Topping:

1 c. ground pecans	1/4 c. brown sugar, packed
1/2 c. sugar	1 t. cinnamon

Mix all ingredients until combined.

Old-fashioned ramekins are ideal for setting out on the breakfast table. Everyone can choose their favorite for toast or bagels when each is filled with a different topping...try jams, jellies, apple or peach butter, marmalade or honey butter.

Delicious Oatmeal Pancakes

June Eier
Forest, OH

My grandchildren simply love these pancakes!

2 c. milk
1-1/2 c. quick-cooking oats,
   uncooked
1 c. all-purpose flour
2-1/2 t. baking powder

1 t. salt
2 T. sugar
2 eggs, beaten
1/3 c. oil

Mix together milk and oats; let stand while sifting together flour, baking powder, salt and sugar in a separate bowl. Stir eggs into oat mixture; mix in dry ingredients and oil. Drop by 1/4 cupfuls onto a hot, lightly greased griddle; flip over when bubbles appear around edges. Cook on each side until lightly golden. Makes 10 to 12 pancakes.

Tuck cheery blossoms inside lots of 1950's-era egg cups and scatter on the breakfast table. They'll make everyone feel perky even before the orange juice is served!

Applesauce Puffs

Jennifer Haugh
Topeka, KS

Dusted with cinnamon and sugar, these will disappear fast!

2 c. biscuit baking mix
1/2 c. sugar, divided
2 t. cinnamon, divided
1/2 c. applesauce

1/4 c. milk
1 egg, beaten
2 T. oil
2 T. butter, melted

Combine biscuit baking mix, 1/4 cup sugar and one teaspoon cinnamon in a mixing bowl; set aside. Mix together applesauce, milk, egg and oil in a separate bowl; pour into dry ingredients. Beat vigorously for 30 seconds. Fill 24 greased muffin tins 2/3 full. Bake at 400 degrees for 12 minutes. Cool in pan for several minutes. Combine remaining sugar and cinnamon in a small bowl. Dip each puff in melted butter then in cinnamon-sugar mixture. Makes 2 dozen.

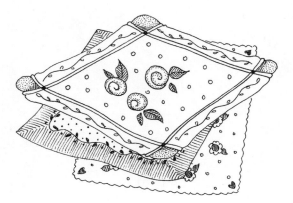

Using Grandma's pretty hankie as a mat for a favorite photo helps little ones remember special times shared together.

French Toast Sticks

Margaret Shelton
Delaware, OH

*Easy for little fingers to pick up, kids like dipping these
in applesauce or warm maple syrup.*

4 to 5 slices bread
3 c. crispy rice cereal, crushed
1 T. sugar
1 t. cinnamon
3 eggs, beaten

1 c. milk
1 t. vanilla extract
1/8 t. salt
4 T. butter, melted

Cut bread into 4 strips each. Combine crushed cereal, sugar and
cinnamon; set aside. In another bowl, mix together eggs, milk, vanilla
and salt. Dip each bread stick into egg mixture and then into sugar
coating. Place sticks in an ungreased 13"x9" baking pan; pour melted
butter over top. Bake at 375 degrees for 15 to 20 minutes until
golden. Makes 16 to 20 sticks.

*Try stuffed French toast
for a new twist! Dip half
the bread slices in egg
mixture and top with
apple butter. Dip the
remaining slices in egg
mixture and lay over
apple butter, pressing
down slightly to make a
"sandwich." Cook on a
hot, oiled griddle until
both sides are
golden...yum!*

Mini Breakfast Cups

Marie Stowers
Jacksonville, FL

This family favorite is a recipe I often make for church breakfasts.
It's a cinch to prepare and bakes in minutes.

2 12-oz. tubes refrigerated
   biscuits
4 to 5 eggs, beaten
1 lb. ground sausage, browned

1 c. shredded Monterey Jack
   cheese
1 c. shredded mild Cheddar
   cheese

Separate each biscuit in half; press into mini muffin tins lightly
sprayed with non-stick vegetable spray. Scramble eggs in a skillet.
Combine eggs, sausage and cheeses. Spoon into muffin tins. Bake at
400 degrees for 7 to 10 minutes until biscuits are golden around
edges. Makes 3 to 4 dozen.

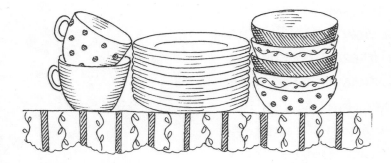

Nostalgic kitchen shelf edging is a snap with a few
scraps of vintage-style wallpaper! Just make color
copies of wallpaper, cut to fit the shelf edge and paste
pieces together. Use decorative-edged scissors to create
a scalloped edge and then tape to shelves.

Apple-Sausage Breakfast Ring

*Gail Hageman
Albion, ME*

*If you'd like, add the sweet taste of maple syrup...just drizzle
each slice before serving.*

2 lbs. ground sausage
2 eggs, beaten
1-1/2 c. round buttery crackers,
   crushed

1 c. apples, cored, peeled
   and grated
1/4 c. milk

Line a Bundt® pan with plastic wrap. Combine all ingredients, mixing
well; press firmly into pan. Chill several hours or overnight. Unmold
onto a jelly roll pan; remove plastic wrap. Bake at 350 degrees for one
hour. Serves 8.

*Look at tag sales and flea markets for fabric
remnants bursting with colorful 1940's fruit
patterns...they make great window toppers.*

Spinach & Bacon Quiche

Barbara Watson
Blountville, TN

Easy to tote, quiche makes an ideal breakfast surprise for new neighbors or a busy mom.

9-inch pie crust
3 eggs, beaten
1 c. half-and-half
1 T. all-purpose flour
1/2 t. salt
10-oz. pkg. frozen chopped
    spinach, thawed and drained

8 slices bacon, crisply cooked
    and crumbled
1/2 c. green onions, chopped
1 c. shredded sharp Cheddar
    cheese
1 c. shredded mozzarella cheese

Fit pie crust into a 9" pie plate. Whisk together eggs, half-and-half, flour and salt. Stir in spinach, bacon, onions and cheeses. Pour mixture into pie crust. Bake at 400 degrees for 15 minutes; reduce temperature to 325 and bake for 30 additional minutes. Cool 5 minutes before serving. Serves 8.

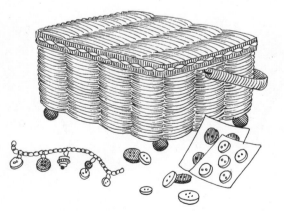

Charms that are cute as a button...sorting through Grandma's sewing box will turn up all sorts of pretty buttons. Dangling from a bracelet's links, they create a sweet, heartfelt charm bracelet.

Make-Ahead Breakfast Eggs

Tamara Wallace
Roscoe, IL

For a wedding shower, my mom created a family cookbook...she asked my grandmothers, sisters, aunts and future in-laws for special recipes and memories. This dish comes from that treasured collection.

12 eggs, beaten
1/2 c. milk
1/2 t. salt
1/4 t. pepper
1 T. butter

1 c. sour cream
12 slices bacon, crisply cooked
   and crumbled
1 c. shredded sharp Cheddar
   cheese

Stir together first 4 ingredients; set aside. In a large skillet, melt butter over medium-low heat. Add egg mixture, stirring occasionally until eggs are set but moist; remove from heat and cool. Stir in sour cream. Spread mixture in a buttered 2-quart shallow baking dish; top with bacon and cheese. Cover dish and refrigerate overnight. Uncover and bake at 300 degrees for 15 to 20 minutes. Serves 6 to 8.

Homestyle Potato Pancakes

Vickie

Golden and crispy!

4 c. mashed potatoes
2 eggs, beaten
2 onions, finely chopped

1 t. salt
1/2 t. pepper
4 T. olive oil

Combine potatoes, eggs and onions in a medium mixing bowl; stir well to blend. Add salt and pepper. Heat oil in a large skillet over medium heat. Drop 1/4 cupfuls potato mixture into oil, flatten each to 3/4-inch thick. Cook each patty until golden on both sides. Makes about 6 servings.

Homemade Granola

Irasema Biggs
Kearney, MO

Enjoy as a hearty, good-for-you cereal, or try it sprinkled on plain or vanilla yogurt.

2 c. quick-cooking oats, uncooked
2 c. whole-grain wheat flake cereal
1/4 c. wheat germ
1 c. walnuts

1 c. sunflower seeds
1 c. raisins
1 c. flaked coconut
1/4 c. butter
1 t. vanilla extract
1/2 c. honey

Combine first 7 ingredients; pour in an ungreased 13"x9" baking pan. Melt together remaining ingredients in a saucepan; pour over granola mixture. Bake at 350 degrees for 20 minutes, stirring after 10 minutes. Makes about 8-1/2 cups.

Don't pass up a discarded window frame without panes...it makes a one-of-a-kind bulletin board. Heavy tacks are ideal for attaching chicken wire to the back of the frame and clothespins will secure photos, notes and special reminders...so clever!

Maimaw's Cinnamon Rolls

Pat Derouen
Gladewater, TX

A recipe handed down from her mother, my mother has made these cinnamon rolls for as long as I can remember.

2 c. all-purpose flour
3 t. baking powder
1 t. salt
1/3 c. shortening

4-3/4 c. milk, divided
1/2 c. sugar
cinnamon to taste
1/4 c. margarine

Sift together flour, baking powder and salt; cut in shortening. Add 3/4 cup milk to form a soft dough. Turn dough onto slightly floured wax paper; knead for 30 seconds to shape. Roll out in a rectangular shape, 1/4-inch thick and sprinkle with sugar and cinnamon; dot with margarine. Roll tightly jelly roll-style and cut into 1/2-inch wide slices; place rolls in a deep roaster pan. Sprinkle any remaining flour, sugar and cinnamon from wax paper on top of rolls; pour remaining milk over top. Bake at 400 degrees for one hour. Makes 12 to 15.

*A grandma is warm hugs and sweet memories.
She is an encouraging word and a tender touch.
She is full of proud smiles.*
-Barbara Cage

English Scones

*Caroline Capper
Circleville, OH*

*This hot, biscuit-style bread is the one I bake most
often...try them with butter and marmalade or jam.*

2 c. all-purpose flour
1/2 t. salt
1 T. baking powder
1/4 c. plus 1 T. sugar, divided
1/4 c. butter

1/4 c. raisins
1/2 c. plus 1 T. whipping cream,
    divided
1 egg, beaten

Mix together flour, salt, baking powder and 1/4 cup sugar; cut in
butter. Fold in raisins, then mix in 1/2 cup cream and egg. Roll dough
into a 3/4-inch thick circle; place on an ungreased baking sheet. Brush
with remaining cream and sprinkle with remaining sugar. Bake at
400 degrees for 15 minutes or until golden. Cut into wedges. Makes
8 servings.

*Share herb cuttings with friends & family...it's a
terrific way to fill a garden with memories.*

Sweet Twists

Mary Jane Tolman
Rocky Mount, NC

All you need to enjoy these is a tall glass of icy milk!

1 pkg. active dry yeast
1/4 c. warm water
3-3/4 c. all-purpose flour
1-1/2 t. salt
1 c. butter

2 eggs, beaten
1/2 c. sour cream
3 t. vanilla extract, divided
1-1/2 c. sugar

Dissolve yeast in water; set aside. Mix flour and salt in a large mixing bowl; cut in butter to resemble coarse crumbs. Blend in eggs, sour cream, one teaspoon vanilla and yeast mixture; cover and chill overnight. Combine sugar and remaining vanilla. Sprinkle 1/2 cup vanilla-sugar mixture on a flat surface; roll out dough on surface to a 16"x8" rectangle. Cut into 4"x1" strips; twist strips and place on greased baking sheets. Bake at 350 degrees for 15 to 20 minutes. Makes 2 dozen.

Show little ones you love them...give 'em hugs & kisses! Cut biscuit or sweet roll dough into X's and O's using alphabet cookie cutters. After baking, brush with melted butter and sprinkle with sugar.

Ham & Egg Brunch Casserole

Candace Elenz
Waverly, IA

While the casserole's baking, slice a variety of fruit...great paired with this cheesy dish.

8 to 10 slices bread, crusts
   trimmed
1 lb. cooked ham, cubed
3/4 c. shredded Cheddar cheese
3/4 c. shredded Swiss cheese

7 to 8 eggs, beaten
2-3/4 c. milk
1 t. dry mustard
1-1/4 t. salt
4 T. butter, melted

Cube bread; place bread and ham in a buttered 13"x9" baking pan. Sprinkle cheeses over top. Combine eggs, milk, mustard and salt; pour over cheese. Pour melted butter over top. Cover and refrigerate overnight. Bake, uncovered, at 325 degrees for one hour or until center tests done. Serves 6 to 8.

Don't pass up a flea market find! A secondhand vinyl tablecloth with a fruit-filled pattern can easily be stitched into a colorful porch swing pillow. Cut out 2 squares, pin right-sides together and stitch along three sides; turn right-side out, slip in a pillow form and hand stitch closed.

Rise & Shine Breakfast Pizza

Micki Stephens
Marion, OH

Tasty layers of all your breakfast favorites!

2-lb. pkg. frozen shredded
    hashbrowns
1-1/2 c. shredded Cheddar
    cheese, divided

7 eggs
1/2 c. milk
salt and pepper to taste
10 to 12 sausage patties, cooked

Prepare hashbrowns according to package directions; spread on an ungreased baking sheet or pizza pan. Top with 1/2 cup cheese; set aside. Whisk eggs and milk together in a microwave-safe bowl; microwave on high for 3 minutes, then scramble eggs well with a whisk. Return to microwave and cook 3 additional minutes; whisk well to scramble. Layer eggs on top of cheese; salt and pepper to taste. Top with remaining cheese. Arrange sausage patties on top. Bake at 400 degrees for 10 minutes or until cheese is melted. Cut into wedges to serve. Serves 8 to 10.

A stepstool is always handy in the kitchen.
Give it personality with a fresh coat of paint, and
then decoupage on color copies of vintage
paper dolls...so sweet!

Nana's Cowboy Coffee Cake

Karen Atchley
Douglasville, GA

This recipe is very special to me. Every holiday or visit from Nana would include the baking of this coffee cake at least once...and it always went quickly.

2-1/4 c. all-purpose flour
1/2 t. salt
2 c. brown sugar, packed
3/4 c. shortening
2 t. baking powder
1/2 t. baking soda
1/2 t. cinnamon
1/2 t. nutmeg
1 c. buttermilk
2 eggs, beaten
Garnish: walnuts

Combine flour, salt, sugar and shortening in a large bowl; mix until crumbly. Set aside 3/4 cup mixture for topping. To the remaining mixture, add baking powder, baking soda, cinnamon and nutmeg; mix in buttermilk and eggs. Pour into a 13"x9" baking pan lined with wax paper. Sprinkle with topping. Lightly press walnuts into batter. Bake at 375 degrees for 25 to 30 minutes. Remove and cool on wire rack. Serves 12 to 15.

Storytelling time! Invite family members to share their most treasured family stories. Be sure to save this special moment by capturing it with a video camera or tape recorder.

Cinnamon-Apple Muffins

Susan Ruppert
Milligan, NE

If you'd like these muffins a little sweeter you can always drizzle them with a simple powdered sugar glaze.

1/2 c. all-purpose flour
1/2 c. powdered milk
1/3 c. sugar
2 t. baking powder
2 t. cinnamon, divided
1/2 t. salt
1 egg

1/2 c. water
1 c. apple, cored, peeled and
   finely chopped
1/4 c. butter, melted
1/3 c. chopped walnuts
1/4 c. brown sugar, packed

Combine flour, milk, sugar, baking powder, 1/2 teaspoon cinnamon and salt in a mixing bowl; set aside. In a separate bowl, beat egg with water; stir in apples and butter. Add apple mixture to dry ingredients, stirring just until moistened; batter will be stiff. Fill 12 buttered muffin cups 2/3 full. Combine nuts, brown sugar and remaining cinnamon; sprinkle over each muffin. Bake at 375 degrees for 15 to 20 minutes. Remove from pan immediately to cool. Makes one dozen.

Take boxes out of storage and display favorite family treasures! Stack old vintage suitcases for a clever end table, frame Grandma's apron and set out Dad's old baseball mitt...they'll bring lots of warm memories and smiles.

Morning Pecan Casserole

Charlotte Peer
Newport, MI

The raisin-cinnamon bread gives this a yummy taste.

8-oz. pkg. sausage patties
16-oz. loaf raisin-cinnamon
   bread, cubed
6 eggs
1-1/2 c. milk
1-1/2 c. half-and-half
1 t. vanilla extract

1/4 t. nutmeg
1/2 t. cinnamon
1 c. brown sugar, packed
1 c. chopped pecans
1/2 c. butter, softened
2 T. maple syrup

Brown sausage patties on both sides over medium-high heat in a skillet; drain off fat and cut into bite-size pieces. Place bread cubes in a 13"x9" baking pan coated with non-stick vegetable spray; top with sausage pieces. In a large mixing bowl, beat together eggs, milk, half-and-half, vanilla, nutmeg and cinnamon; pour over bread and sausage, pressing sausage and bread into egg mixture. Cover and refrigerate 8 hours or overnight. In a separate bowl, combine brown sugar, pecans, butter and syrup; drop by teaspoonfuls over casserole. Bake at 350 degrees for 35 to 40 minutes or until center tests done. Serves 8 to 10.

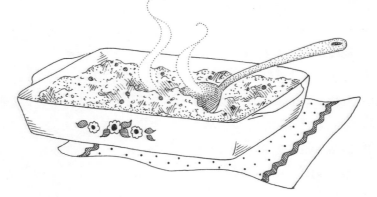

grandma's have bottomless handbags.
-Unknown

Old-Fashioned Oatmeal

Wendy Lane
Quaker City, OH

Great for a chilly morning...this'll warm you head to toe!

1/2 c. oil
2 eggs
1 c. sugar
3 c. quick-cooking oats,
    uncooked

2 t. baking powder
1 t. salt
1 c. milk

Combine oil, eggs and sugar. Add oats, baking powder, salt and milk. Pour into a lightly greased 1-1/2 quart baking dish. Bake at 350 degrees for 45 minutes. Makes 4 servings.

A well-worn garden hat and a sprinkling can that belonged to Grandma can bring back many happy memories. Nestle them in a jelly cupboard with lots of family photos to create a memory-filled corner that says "Welcome Home."

Strawberry French Toast

Patricia Nazaruk
Michigan Center, MI

Tastes like strawberry cheesecake!

8-oz. container ricotta cheese
3 T. powdered sugar
1 t. vanilla extract
16 slices French bread or
    Texas toast

2 eggs
1 c. milk
Garnish: sliced strawberries and
    powdered sugar

In a small bowl, combine ricotta, sugar and vanilla. Spread
2 tablespoons mix onto 8 slices bread; top with remaining bread to
make 8 sandwiches. In a separate bowl, beat eggs and milk together.
Soak sandwiches in milk mixture one to 2 minutes on each side. Cook
on a hot, greased griddle for 3 to 5 minutes on each side or until
golden. Top with strawberries and powdered sugar. Makes
8 sandwiches.

*Keep an eye open for those great milk pitchers like
grandma used to have...shaped like a rooster or cow,
they add a spark of fun to any breakfast table!*

Apple Pancakes with Cider Sauce

Carol Hickman
Kingsport, TN

The cider sauce makes these pancakes out of this world!

2 c. buttermilk biscuit
   baking mix
1/2 t. cinnamon
1 egg, beaten

1-1/3 c. milk
2 apples, cored, peeled
   and grated

Blend together all ingredients. Drop by 1/4 cupfuls onto a hot, buttered griddle; cook on both sides until golden. Serve with sauce. Makes 18 pancakes.

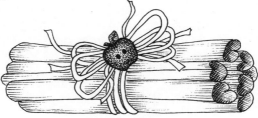

Cider Sauce:

1 c. sugar
2 T. cornstarch
1/2 t. cinnamon
1/4 t. nutmeg

2 c. apple cider
2 T. lemon juice
1/4 c. butter

Mix together sugar, cornstarch, cinnamon and nutmeg in a saucepan; stir in cider and lemon juice. Cook over medium heat, stirring constantly, until mixture thickens and boils. Boil and stir for one minute. Remove from heat; stir in butter until melted.

Pancake breakfasts are a favorite small town gathering. Look in the newspaper to see if there's one planned at a local grange hall or church and make plans to go.

Hashbrown Bake

Michelle Alexander
Boonville, IN

Any way you like your eggs, you can be sure that, paired up with these golden, cheesy potatoes, you'll have a winning combination.

2-lb. pkg. frozen shredded
    hashbrowns
salt and pepper to taste
1/2 c. onion, chopped
1 c. sour cream

10-3/4 oz. can cream of chicken
    soup
3 c. shredded Cheddar cheese
1/2 c. butter

Place hashbrowns in a greased 13"x9" baking pan; salt and pepper to taste. In a mixing bowl, combine onion, sour cream and soup; pour over potatoes. Sprinkle with cheese, then dot with butter. Bake at 350 degrees for one hour or until top becomes golden. Serves 6 to 8.

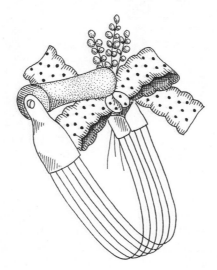

Copies of handwritten recipe cards make an ideal cover for a family cookbook. Attach them with spray adhesive and then fill the book with the family's best-loved recipes!

HEARTY SOUPS & HOMEY BAKED breads

Homemade Chicken Noodle Soup

Francie Stutzman
Dalton, OH

Chicken Noodle Soup is magic...well, at least it seems to be.
Whenever we're feeling under the weather and looking for
old-fashioned comfort, this is a staple we can count on.

2 c. all-purpose flour
1 egg
2 egg yolks
2 t. salt

1/2 c. water
1/4 c. butter
2 10-1/2 oz. cans chicken broth
2 5-oz. cans chicken

Mix together flour, egg, egg yolks, salt and water. Turn dough out onto
a floured surface; roll dough to less than 1/8-inch thickness. Cut
dough into one-inch strips; set aside. Combine butter and broth in a
stockpot; bring to a boil. Carefully drop noodles into broth. Reduce
temperature to low; cook until noodles rise to the top, about
15 minutes. Add chicken and heat through. Makes about 4 servings.

Other things may change us,
but we start and end with family.
-Anthony Brandt

Alabama Biscuits

Teresa Stiegelmeyer
Indianapolis, IN

When visiting my grandparents on the farm, Grandma would make these biscuits. I always loved to watch her, so she would stand me on a chair and tie a tea towel around me as an apron!

4 T. sugar
1 t. baking soda
1 t. salt
5 c. all-purpose flour
1 c. shortening

2 pkgs. active dry yeast
2 c. room temperature
  buttermilk
1 c. butter, melted

Mix sugar, baking soda, salt and flour together; cut in shortening. Dissolve yeast in buttermilk; add to sugar mixture. Knead dough; roll out to 1/4-inch thick. Cut with a biscuit cutter. Dip each roll in melted butter; sandwich 2 biscuits together. Place biscuits on a lightly greased baking sheet. Let dough rise in a warm place until double in bulk. Bake at 325 degrees for 15 to 20 minutes. Makes about 2 dozen.

Try making bread from scratch...it's a terrific way to say "I love you" to family & friends and the aroma is impossible to resist!

Sausage & Corn Chowder

Holly Dodds
Greenville, TX

If you have a garden, save some corn just for this recipe.

1 onion, chopped
1/2 c. margarine, divided
1 lb. Kielbasa, diced
1 lb. new potatoes, peeled
   and cubed
2 stalks celery, chopped
1 qt. chicken broth

2 c. corn
1 qt. half-and-half
1/2 t. baking soda
3 T. all-purpose flour
salt and pepper to taste
Garnish: fresh parsley, chopped

Sauté onion in 1/4 cup margarine in a large saucepan. Add kielbasa;
cook until browned. Stir in potatoes, celery and broth; bring to a boil.
Add corn, half-and-half and baking soda; simmer for 10 minutes and
set aside. In a separate saucepan, melt remaining margarine; add flour.
Stir for 2 minutes; whisk into soup. Season with salt and pepper.
Garnish with parsley before serving. Serves 6 to 8.

A child's old metal truck makes a terrific key and
mail caddy...it's roomy enough for lots of letters
and adds a touch of whimsy!

Baked Potato Soup

Jill Williams
Hiawatha, KS

What a wonderful soup! Thick, creamy and garnished with crisp bacon, it's terrific served with thick slices of homemade bread.

2/3 c. butter
2/3 c. all-purpose flour
3/4 t. salt
1/4 t. white pepper
6 c. milk
1 c. sour cream

4 potatoes, baked, peeled
  and cubed
1/4 c. green onions, sliced
10 slices bacon, crisply cooked
  and crumbled
1 c. shredded Cheddar cheese

Melt butter in a large stockpot; stir in flour, salt and pepper. Pour in milk; bring to a boil. Continue cooking for 2 minutes, stirring constantly. Remove from heat; whisk in sour cream. Add potatoes and onions. Top with bacon and cheese before serving. Serves 8 to 10.

A collection of delicate paper dolls can be a challenge to protect and yet enjoy. Framing them easily solves the problem...so sweet in a little girl's room!

Banana-Nut Bread

Renae Scheiderer
Beallsville, OH

Always a favorite and oh-so easy to make.

2 c. all-purpose flour
1/2 t. baking powder
1/2 t. baking soda
1/2 t. salt
1/2 c. butter

1 c. sugar
2 eggs
3 bananas, mashed
1/2 c. chopped nuts

Mix all ingredients together; pour into a greased 9"x5" baking pan. Bake at 350 degrees for 45 to 60 minutes. Makes 6 to 8 servings.

Monie's Apple Bread

Connie Bell
Arlington, TN

Top with softened cream cheese for a real treat.

1-1/3 c. all-purpose flour
3/4 t. baking soda
1/2 t. salt
1/2 t. cinnamon
1/2 t. ground cloves
1/2 c. oil
1 c. sugar

2 eggs
1 t. vanilla extract
2 apples, cored, peeled
    and chopped
1/2 c. chopped nuts
1/2 c. raisins

Combine first 5 ingredients; set aside. Mix together oil, sugar, eggs and vanilla. Add apples, nuts and raisins; stir in flour mixture, blending well. Pour into a greased and floured 9"x5" loaf pan; bake at 325 degrees for one hour. Makes 6 to 8 servings.

Apple-Barley Soup

Jo Ann

Fresh apples give color and a slightly sweet taste to this recipe.

2 onions, thinly sliced
2 T. oil
3-1/2 c. vegetable broth
1-1/2 c. apple cider
1/3 c. pearled barley, uncooked
2 carrots, diced
1 t. dried thyme
1/4 t. dried marjoram
1 bay leaf
2 c. apples, cored and chopped
1/4 c. fresh parsley, minced
1 T. lemon juice
1/4 t. salt

Sauté onions in oil over medium heat in a small stockpot. Reduce heat; cover and cook 10 minutes, stirring occasionally, until browned. Add broth, cider, barley, carrots, thyme, marjoram and bay leaf. Cover and cook one hour until barley is tender. Combine remaining ingredients in a small bowl, then add to soup; cook 5 minutes until apples are tender. Discard bay leaf before serving. Makes 4 to 6 servings.

An old enamel saucepan will keep garden twine handy while tying up and staking plants. The twine inside rolls around but doesn't tangle and the handle makes it easy to grab & go!

Grandma's Fluffy Dinner Rolls

Penny Mixon
Humble, TX

*There's just something about homemade rolls, warm from the oven
and spread with butter, that make any meal better.*

2 pkgs. active dry yeast
3 c. warm water
2/3 c. sugar
6 T. oil

1/8 t. salt
7-1/2 c. all-purpose flour
3 T. butter, melted

Dissolve yeast in water. Add sugar, oil and salt to yeast mixture; stir
until sugar dissolves. Sift in flour; mix well. Cover dough; let rise one
to 1-1/2 hours or until double in bulk. Turn out dough onto a floured
surface; knead for 7 minutes. Cut dough into one-inch size balls; place
on an aluminum foil-lined baking sheet. Cover with with plastic wrap
that has been sprayed with non-stick vegetable spray; let rolls rise
30 to 40 minutes. Bake at 375 degrees for 12 minutes; reduce to
350 degrees. Bake an additional 10 minutes. Brush tops with melted
butter before serving. Makes 2 dozen.

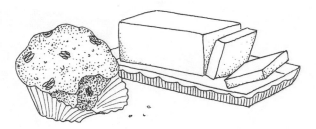

*Try making flavored butter to spread on warm
biscuits or bread...it makes them extra special and it's
so easy. Just blend fresh, minced herbs to taste with
softened butter, cover and then chill at least
2 to 3 hours so the flavors will blend.*

French Onion Soup

Andrea Pocreva
Navarre, FL

A classic...serve immediately for the best flavor.

5 onions, thinly sliced
1/3 c. butter
2 T. all-purpose flour
3 10-1/2 oz. cans beef broth
water

1/2 t. pepper
1-1/2 c. grated Parmesan cheese
6 slices bread
12 slices Swiss cheese

Sauté onions in butter in a small saucepan. Stir in flour, whisking until smooth; pour mixture into a large stockpot. Stir in broth, 2 broth cans of water and pepper. Cover; cook on low for 30 minutes. In each individual bowl, cover bottom with Parmesan cheese, fill each with soup, then top each with one slice of bread and 2 slices Swiss cheese. Place bowls on a baking sheet; broil until cheese is melted. Serves 6.

Show off a collection of glass juicers or pie birds by lining them up on a kitchen shelf. Found in lots of colors and sizes, they're practical and pretty!

Beef-Vegetable Soup

Kelley Girtz
Becker, MN

Make up a large batch over the weekend and freeze for quick meals throughout the week.

1 lb. ground beef
1 T. dried, minced onion
1 t. garlic, minced
28-oz. can chopped tomatoes
6 c. water
2 T. lemon juice
2 T. balsamic vinegar

4 cubes beef bouillon
1 c. corn
1 c. carrots, chopped
1 c. peas
salt and pepper to taste
1/2 c. orzo pasta, uncooked

Brown beef, onion and garlic in a large skillet; drain. Combine all ingredients in a large stockpot; simmer 30 minutes. Serves 6 to 8.

Bring best-loved family photos to life! Type a quote or clever phrase on the computer, print it on vellum and slip it under the frame glass next to the photo. A first birthday picture might say "Make a wish!" while a family reunion snapshot might say "The whole kin & kaboodle!"

Cheddar-Garlic Biscuits

Debbie Rieder
Staunton, VA

*Even if you love to spend time in the kitchen, you'll appreciate
how quickly these biscuits can be made.*

2-1/2 c. biscuit baking mix
1 c. shredded Cheddar cheese
3/4 c. milk
1/8 t. garlic powder

1/4 c. plus 2 T. butter, melted
  and divided
1/2 t. garlic salt
1/2 t. dried parsley

Combine baking mix, cheese, milk, garlic powder and 2 tablespoons
butter; mix well. Form 1/4 cup mixture into a ball; place on an
ungreased baking sheet. Repeat with remaining mixture. Bake at
400 degrees for 14 to 16 minutes. Mix together remaining butter,
garlic salt and parsley; brush over biscuits before serving. Makes
12 to 16.

*Create a terrific shadowbox that's full of memories!
Choose a favorite photo and match it with goodies
tucked away in drawers and boxes. For example a
photo taken at the beach paired with a few seashells
or Mom & Dad's wedding picture with a paper
valentine tucked alongside.*

Beef & Black-Eyed Pea Soup

Paula Ramey
Hopkinsville, KY

This soup is delicious on a cold day with warm, buttered cornbread. We enjoy it on New Year's Day to bring us good luck all year.

2 lbs. ground beef
1/2 c. green pepper, chopped
1/2 c. butter
1/2 c. all-purpose flour
2 qts. water
28-oz. can chopped tomatoes
16-oz. pkg. frozen black-eyed
    peas
1 c. onion, chopped

1 c. carrots, diced
1 c. celery, chopped
2 T. beef bouillon granules
1 T. pepper
1/2 t. salt
1/4 t. garlic powder
1/4 t. onion powder
1-1/2 c. prepared rice

Brown beef and green pepper in a skillet; drain. Melt butter in a Dutch oven; add flour, whisking until smooth. Cook one minute, stirring constantly. Gradually add water; stir until bubbly. Stir in beef mixture and all remaining ingredients, except rice. Bring to a boil; cover and simmer 45 minutes to one hour. Add rice during last 15 minutes. Serves 6 to 8.

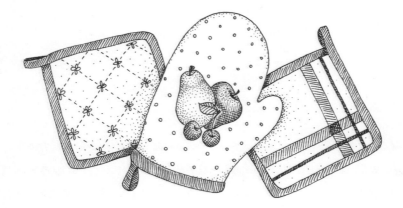

The family is one of nature's masterpieces.
-George Santayana

Rye Bread

Karen Anderson
Stockholm, ME

This recipe makes a light, moist loaf of bread...yummy for sandwiches!

1 T. active dry yeast
2 T. plus 1/8 t. brown sugar,
   packed and divided
2 c. warm water, divided
2 T. molasses

2 T. shortening
1 t. salt
1 T. anise seed, crushed
5 c. bread flour, divided
2 c. rye flour

Dissolve yeast and 1/8 teaspoon brown sugar in 1/4 cup warm water; set aside. In a separate bowl, combine remaining warm water, brown sugar, molasses, shortening and salt; add anise seed and allow mixture to cool. Once cool, stir in 2 cups bread flour and yeast mixture. Mix in rye flour. Gradually add enough remaining bread flour to form a soft dough. Turn dough out onto a lightly floured surface; knead about 10 minutes. Place dough in a greased bowl, cover and let rise in a warm place until double in bulk. Divide dough in half and place each half in a greased 9"x5" baking pan; let rise. Bake at 350 degrees for 20 minutes. Cover loaves with aluminum foil; bake 20 additional minutes. Serves 12 to 15.

Pressing flowers from Grandma's garden is a beautiful way to preserve memories...decoupage them on a book mark or slip beneath the glass on a picture frame.

Potato & Cheddar Soup

Delinda Blakney
Bridgeview, IL

Truly delicious…thick and filling. If you'd like, garnish with some fresh chives or scallions for added flavor and color.

1/4 c. butter, melted
1 lb. potatoes, peeled and cubed
2 stalks celery, chopped
1 onion, chopped
1 t. paprika
2 c. milk

13-3/4 oz. can chicken broth
1 c. water
1 t. salt
1/4 t. pepper
10-oz. pkg. shredded sharp
    Cheddar cheese

Combine butter, potatoes, celery and onion in a large saucepan; cook for 10 minutes. Stir in paprika; cook one additional minute. Add milk, broth, water, salt and pepper; bring to a boil. Simmer for 20 minutes; remove from heat. Stir cheese into hot soup until melted. Serves 6 to 8.

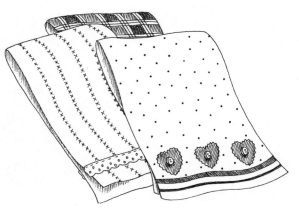

Fill a shelf with inexpensive trinkets and give any room an instant vintage feel. Look for tiny glass bottles, kitchen gadgets, thread spools or button cards. Even skeleton keys can still be found at family-owned hardware stores.

Chicken-Tortellini Soup

Denise Iannuzzi
Raynham, MA

When I'm in a pinch for time, I use rotisserie chicken from
a local grocery store...already cooked!

3 to 4-lb. chicken, cooked and
    skin removed
5 8-oz. cans chicken broth
6 carrots, peeled and sliced
1 onion, chopped
3 stalks celery, chopped

1/8 t. fresh rosemary
1 clove garlic, minced
salt and pepper to taste
7-oz. pkg. rainbow cheese
    tortellini, uncooked

Cube chicken and place in a large stockpot; add the next 7 ingredients.
Bring to a boil. Add tortellini; simmer according to package directions.
Serves 6 to 8.

Childhood party games make it easy for long-lost
relatives to enjoy a reunion while getting to know
each other. Turn a tried & true favorite like
Pin the Tail on the Donkey into
Pin the Beard on Uncle Merle!

Lemon Bread

Laurie Murphy
LaPlata, MD

To really perk up the flavor and add more tartness, just substitute one teaspoon of minced fresh lemon balm for the lemon zest.

1-1/2 c. all-purpose flour
1 t. baking powder
1/2 t. salt
6 T. shortening
1-1/3 c. sugar, divided

2 eggs, beaten
1 T. lemon zest
1/2 c. milk
3 T. lemon juice

Mix together flour, baking powder and salt; set aside. Cream together shortening and one cup sugar; add eggs and lemon zest. Stir into flour mixture alternately with milk. Pour into a greased and floured 8-1/2"x4-1/2" baking pan; bake at 350 degrees for one hour or until center tests done. Dissolve remaining sugar in lemon juice; pour over bread. Remove from pan to cool. Makes 6 to 8 servings.

Vintage button cards add a sweet touch to a plain notecard. Form a mat by cutting a piece of fabric slightly larger than the button card and secure them together with spray adhesive. Use adhesive again to attach both to the front of the notecard.

Hazel's Pumpkin Bread

Angela Stevens
South Point, OH

This recipe was passed down to me from my grandmother. Adding candied cherries makes pumpkin bread even more delightful.

1-2/3 c. all-purpose flour	1/2 c. oil
1-1/4 c. sugar	2 eggs
1 t. baking soda	1 c. canned pumpkin
1/2 t. cinnamon	1/3 c. water
1/2 t. nutmeg	1/2 c. candied cherries, halved
1/4 t. salt	1/2 c. chopped nuts

Combine first 6 ingredients in a large mixing bowl; set aside. In a separate bowl, mix together oil, eggs, pumpkin and water. Add pumpkin mixture to dry ingredients; mix well. Fold in cherries and nuts. Pour mixture into a greased and floured 9"x5" baking pan. Bake at 350 degrees for one hour or until center tests done. Makes 6 to 8 servings.

When hosting a reunion, give everyone a giggle by greeting them at the door with a photo wreath! Color copy snapshots of family members and punch holes at the top of each. Slip a length of ribbon through and tie onto a grapevine wreath.

Beefy Wild Rice Soup

Cristy Koker
Racine, WI

Served with a crusty loaf of bread, this soup is a meal!

2 qts. water
3 T. beef bouillon granules
1 T. onion soup mix
2 14-1/2 oz. cans chopped
    tomatoes
1-1/2 c. stew beef, cooked
    and cubed
2 stalks celery, chopped

1 c. cabbage, shredded
3/4 c. dried lentils
1/2 c. frozen mixed vegetables
1/4 c. catsup
1 T. instant wild rice, uncooked
2 cloves garlic, minced
1/2 t. hot pepper sauce
1/2 t. pepper

Combine all ingredients in a large stockpot. Bring soup to a boil.
Reduce heat, cover and simmer 50 to 55 minutes. Serves 8.

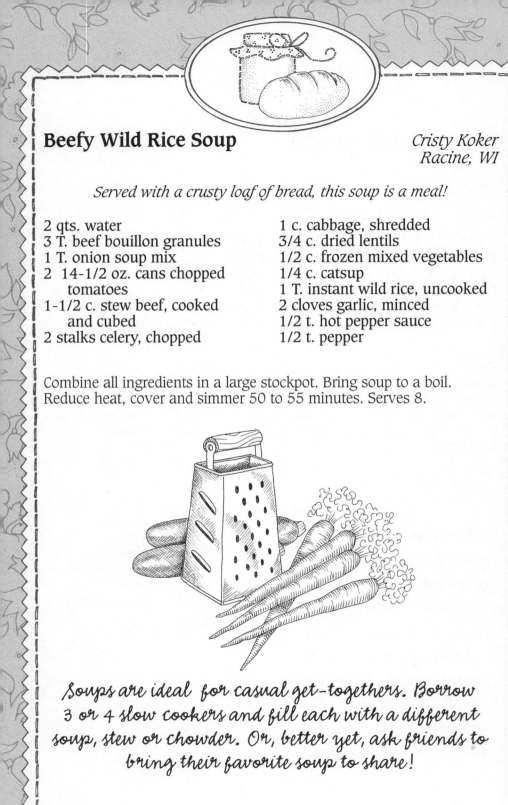

*Soups are ideal for casual get-togethers. Borrow
3 or 4 slow cookers and fill each with a different
soup, stew or chowder. Or, better yet, ask friends to
bring their favorite soup to share!*

Sunday Dinner Potato Rolls

Mary Murray
Gooseberry Patch

Growing up, Sunday dinner was the most important meal in our home, and these rolls were always served fresh from the oven.

2 pkgs. active dry yeast
2 c. warm water
1/2 c. sugar
1-1/4 T. salt
1 c. warm mashed potatoes

1/2 c. butter, softened
2 eggs
7-1/2 c. all-purpose flour,
  divided
3 T. butter, melted

Dissolve yeast in water; add sugar, salt, potatoes, butter and eggs. Gradually beat in 3-1/2 cups flour; continue beating for 2 minutes. Mix in remaining flour; knead dough several strokes. Coat dough with melted butter; place in a bowl and refrigerate 2 hours. Punch down; refrigerate overnight. Punch down and knead. Divide dough in half; shape each half into 24 rolls. Place rolls on lightly greased baking sheets; let dough rise in a warm place. Bake at 325 degrees for 40 minutes. Makes 4 dozen rolls.

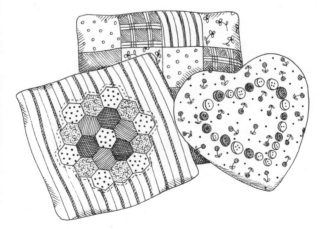

pretty embroidered linens or colorful tea towels draped over a curtain rod seem to instantly make a room feel like home.

Country Cornbread

Rachel Anderson
Livermore, CA

*Pour the batter into old-fashioned
corn-shaped pans...the kids will love 'em!*

1 c. all-purpose flour
1 c. cornmeal
4 t. baking powder
1/2 t. baking soda
2 t. salt

1 egg
1-1/2 c. buttermilk
6 T. butter, melted, cooled
   and divided
1 T. sugar

Preheat an 8" cast iron skillet in a 425-degree oven. While skillet is heating, combine first 5 ingredients in a mixing bowl. Stir in egg, buttermilk, 4 tablespoons butter and sugar. Remove skillet from oven and brush with remaining melted butter; pour batter into skillet. Return to oven and bake at 425 degrees for 15 to 20 minutes. Serves 4 to 6.

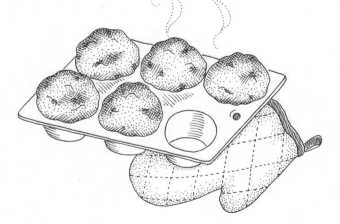

Add a delicious surprise to a favorite cornbread recipe...try fresh corn, chopped green chilies or red peppers, crumbled bacon or chives.

Spicy Chili

Anna Babel
Westerville, OH

An all-time favorite!

3-3/4 T. oil	3-3/4 c. chicken broth
2 onions, chopped	1/3 c. tomato paste
1 clove garlic, minced	1-1/4 t. dried oregano
1 chili pepper, chopped	1 bay leaf
1-1/4 T. paprika	1/4 c. water
1/2 lb. ground beef	salt and pepper to taste
28-oz. can chopped tomatoes	1-1/2 c. kidney beans

Heat oil in a large saucepan. Add onions and garlic; sauté until soft.
Stir in chili pepper and paprika; cook for 30 seconds. Stir in beef; cook
until browned. Add tomatoes, chicken broth, tomato paste, oregano,
bay leaf, water, salt and pepper; bring to a boil. Cover and simmer for
35 minutes. Add beans and simmer 15 additional minutes. Discard
bay leaf before serving. Makes 4 servings.

Soups sometimes spill, so keep lots of bandannas on
hand...they make great lap-size napkins too!

Ham, Bean & Potato Soup

Mary Beth Rykala
Johnstown, PA

You'll find yourself passing this recipe on from friend to friend.

2 c. diced ham
3 to 4 potatoes, peeled
  and chopped
6 c. water
14-1/2 oz. can green beans,
  drained

1 T. chicken bouillon granules
1/4 c. shortening
1/3 c. all-purpose flour
1 t. browning and
  seasoning sauce

Combine ham, potatoes and water in a large pot. Bring to a boil and heat until potatoes are tender. Add green beans and bouillon. In a skillet, melt shortening; whisk in flour until well blended. Add to boiling soup; quickly stir until soup thickens. Stir in seasoning sauce. Serves 4 to 6.

Try some soup toppers to make a favorite recipe even better...grated cheese, chow mein noodles, diced green peppers, toasted nuts or chopped herbs.

Cream of Broccoli Soup

Dee Ice
Delaware, OH

Add a cup of cheese or diced, cooked chicken for a whole new flavor.

1 bunch broccoli, chopped
1 onion, chopped
4 c. chicken broth
4 T. butter

1/2 c. all-purpose flour
2 c. milk
salt, pepper and garlic powder
  to taste

Simmer broccoli and onion in broth in a large stockpot until tender, about 10 to 12 minutes. In a separate saucepan, melt butter; whisk in flour. Add milk; cook until thickened. Whisk milk mixture into broccoli mixture; simmer for 5 to 10 additional minutes. Serves 6.

Homemade vegetable broth is so easy and gives soup a really fresh flavor. Place a variety of vegetables in a stockpot, cover with water and cook for 30 minutes. The broth can be frozen until it's needed and the vegetables can be used in any recipe.

Dakota Bread

Margaret Scoresby
Mount Vernon, OH

Mom always has this hearty bread waiting in the cupboard when we visit. It's named for all the good grains in it, which are grown in the Dakotas.

1 pkg. active dry yeast
1/2 c. warm water
2 T. oil
1 egg
1/2 c. cottage cheese
1/4 c. honey
1 t. salt
2 to 3 c. bread flour, divided
1/2 c. whole-wheat flour
1/4 c. wheat germ
1/4 c. rye flour
1/4 c. long-cooking oats, uncooked
1/8 c. cornmeal
1 egg white, beaten
1/8 c. sunflower seeds

Mix yeast and water together in a small bowl; stir to dissolve and set aside. In a large bowl, mix together oil, egg, cottage cheese, honey and salt. Add yeast mixture and 2 cups bread flour, beating until smooth. Gradually stir in whole-wheat flour, wheat germ, rye flour and oats. Add enough remaining bread flour to make a soft dough. Knead dough on a lightly floured surface until smooth and elastic. Place in an oiled bowl; cover and let rise until double in bulk. Punch dough down. Shape into one round loaf and place in a pie pan coated with non-stick vegetable spray and sprinkled with cornmeal. Cover with oiled plastic wrap and let dough rise again until double in bulk. Brush with egg white and sprinkle with sunflower seeds. Bake at 350 degrees for 35 to 40 minutes. Cool on a wire rack. Makes 6 to 8 servings.

A collection of mismatched game pieces really perk up picture frames! Glue on checkers and dice, or use glue to attach Scrabble® letters to spell out names.

Creamy Vegetable Chowder

Amanda Neelley
Spring Hill, TN

You'll like this twist on the usual vegetable soup.

1 bunch green onions, chopped
4 T. butter
5 c. chicken broth
2 c. powdered non-dairy
   creamer

2 carrots, peeled and sliced
2 potatoes, peeled and sliced
1/4 c. instant rice, uncooked
10-oz. pkg. frozen chopped
   broccoli, thawed

Sauté onions in butter in a large saucepan. Stir in broth and creamer; mix well. Add carrots, potatoes and rice; simmer 15 minutes. Add broccoli. Simmer an additional 15 minutes. Serves 4 to 6.

Buttery Mustard Spread

Janet Pastrick
Gooseberry Patch

Serve with warm bread or over vegetables for extra flavor.

1/2 c. Dijon mustard
1/2 c. butter, softened

1 clove garlic, pressed

Blend together all ingredients. Refrigerate until ready to serve. Makes one cup.

Snap up milk glass tabletop sets, straw dispensers or whimsical salt & pepper shakers when you spot them...so nostalgic!

Mom's Popovers

Jennifer Dutcher
Gooseberry Patch

Traditionally served with roast, these light and puffy breads are sure to be a hit.

5 T. butter
4 eggs

1 c. all-purpose flour
1 c. milk

Divide butter equally between 10 muffin pan cups. Place in a 425-degree oven until butter is melted. Beat eggs until foamy; add flour and milk. Continue to beat for one minute. Pour batter into muffin cups, filling them 3/4 full. Bake at 425 degrees for 10 minutes. Reduce oven temperature to 350 degrees and continue to bake for 10 additional minutes. Don't open oven door. Makes 10 servings.

Scour tag sales for the big, old-fashioned enamelware stockpots. They're just the right size for family-size portions of soups, stews and chowders.

Cheesy Chicken Soup

Kristina Johnson
Quitman, TX

Easy to make and simply delicious!

1 onion, chopped
1 T. butter
16-oz. pkg. pasteurized process
   cheese spread, cubed
10-3/4 oz. can cream of
   mushroom soup

10-3/4 oz. can cream of
   chicken soup
2 8-oz. cans chicken broth
2 10-oz. cans chicken
10-oz. can diced tomatoes
   with chilies

Sauté onion in butter in a saucepan until soft. Add all remaining ingredients; simmer for one hour. Serves 4 to 6.

Potato-Corn Chowder

Jennifer Capellen
Bountiful, UT

Filled to the brim with vegetables!

10-3/4 oz. can cream of
   chicken soup
16-oz. pkg. pasteurized process
   cheese spread, cubed
3-1/2 c. chicken broth

4 potatoes, baked, peeled
   and cubed
15-1/4 oz. can corn
10-oz. pkg. frozen mixed
   vegetables

Combine all ingredients in a stockpot. Heat on medium-low, stirring to combine. Continue cooking until heated though, about 30 to 45 minutes. Serves 4 to 6.

Capture heartfelt memories in a family scrapbook by tucking corrugated paper hearts throughout...they can even be tied with a sheer ribbon or a raffia bow.

Mexican Meatball Soup

Michelle Serrano
Ramona, CA

Tasty meatballs in a tomato-beef broth.

3/4 lb. ground beef
3/4 lb. ground pork
1/3 c. instant rice, uncooked
1-1/2 t. salt
1/4 t. pepper
1 egg, beaten

1 T. fresh mint, chopped
1 onion, minced
1 clove garlic, minced
1 T. oil
10-3/4 oz. can tomato soup
3 qts. beef broth

Mix together beef, pork, rice, salt, pepper, egg and mint; shape into one-inch balls and set aside. In a large stockpot, sauté onion and garlic in oil; add tomato soup and beef broth. Heat until boiling; place meatballs in broth. Cover; cook 30 minutes. Serves 6 to 8.

When making homemade broth, freeze it in ice cube trays. Once they're frozen, slip them into a plastic zipping bag and return to the freezer...a convenient way to add just the amount needed to any soup!

Parmesan-Garlic Bread

Roxanne Bixby
West Franklin, NH

So easy, why not make it at home?

1/2 pt. whipping cream
1/4 c. mayonnaise
9 cloves garlic, minced
3/4 c. plus 2 T. grated Parmesan
    cheese, divided

1 loaf French bread, sliced
paprika to taste

Whip whipping cream until thick; blend in mayonnaise. Add garlic and 3/4 cup Parmesan cheese; stir well. Slice French bread in half lengthwise; generously spread garlic mixture on each half. Sprinkle with remaining Parmesan cheese and paprika. Place loaf halves on an ungreased baking sheet; bake at 400 degrees for 15 to 20 minutes until garlic topping turns golden. Cut into one-inch slices. Makes about 2 dozen slices.

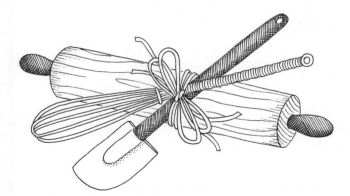

Celebrate Good Neighbor Day, September 28, by sharing a big basket of freshly baked bread with neighbors. They'll love it!

New England Clam Chowder

Patti Willhardt
Merritt Island, FL

*When time allows, try making this with
fresh clams...you'll need about 30.*

1 c. butter
3/4 c. scallions, chopped
2 8-oz. pkgs. cream cheese,
   softened
4 10-3/4 oz. cans potato soup
2 14-3/4 oz. cans creamed corn
4 6-1/2 oz. cans minced clams,
   drained and rinsed

milk
1 to 2 lbs. shrimp, deveined
   and cleaned
salt and pepper to taste
Garnish: shredded Cheddar
   cheese

Melt butter in a large stockpot; add scallions and stir in cream cheese.
Add soup, corn and clams. Stir in milk to desired consistency. Add
shrimp and cook until pink. Salt and pepper to taste. Top with cheese
before serving. Makes 8 to 10 servings.

*Making croutons at home is easy, so why not try?
Cube 4 slices of bread and place in a shallow baking
pan. Combine 3 tablespoons melted butter with
1/4 teaspoon garlic powder and toss with bread.
Bake for 30 minutes in a 300-degree oven.*

Slow-Cooker Beef Stew

Sherri Hagel
Spokane, WA

*Great for a busy day...just toss soup ingredients in the
slow cooker and forget about it!*

4 T. all-purpose flour
1 t. onion powder
1/2 t. salt
1/4 t. pepper
1 lb. stew beef, cubed
2 T. olive oil
46-oz. can tomato juice
2 onions, chopped

4 stalks celery, chopped
1 bay leaf
4 carrots, chopped
3 potatoes, peeled and cubed
1 c. frozen green beans
6 to 8 cubes beef bouillon
1-1/2 c. water

Combine flour, onion powder, salt and pepper in a large plastic zipping
bag; shake to mix. Add beef to bag; shake to coat. Heat olive oil in a
skillet; add beef and brown on all sides. Place beef in a slow cooker;
add tomato juice just until beef is covered. Add onions, celery and bay
leaf. Cook beef on low until tender, about 4 to 6 hours. Add carrots,
potatoes, green beans, bouillon and water; cook one to 2 hours until
vegetables are tender. Serves 4 to 6.

*Start tonight's dinner
early and then forget
about it...the handy
warm setting on the
slow cooker keeps
food just right for
serving. Ideal for
potlucks or
carry-ins too.*

Cranberry-Orange Bread

Karen Rawson
Elkins, WV

Almost like a tea bread, it's terrific spread with cream cheese.

2 c. all-purpose flour
1 c. sugar
1-1/2 t. baking powder
1/2 t. baking soda
3/4 c. orange juice
1 T. orange zest

2 T. shortening
1 egg, beaten
1/2 c. chopped nuts
1/2 c. raisins
1-1/2 c. cranberries, chopped

Mix together flour, sugar, baking powder and baking soda; stir in orange juice, orange zest, shortening and egg. Add nuts, raisins and cranberries; pour into a greased 9"x5" loaf pan. Bake at 350 degrees for 50 minutes. Makes 6 to 8 servings.

Quick breads paired with a cup of steaming herbal tea seem to say "Make yourself at home." Call a friend, invite her over and then kick off your shoes and spend some time catching up.

Zucchini & Walnut Bread

Dawn Menard
Seekonk, MA

*The flavor of this classic quick bread is just right with a
hint of cinnamon and the crunch of walnuts.*

3 eggs
2 c. sugar
1 c. oil
2 c. zucchini, grated
2 c. all-purpose flour
1/4 t. baking powder

2 t. baking soda
1 t. salt
3 t. cinnamon
1 t. vanilla extract
1/2 c. chopped walnuts

Beat together eggs, sugar, oil and zucchini in a large mixing
bowl; add remaining ingredients. Pour into 2 greased and floured
3-3/4"x2-1/2" mini loaf pans. Bake at 350 degrees for one hour or
until inserted toothpick comes out clean. Makes 2 loaves.

*Look for oilcloth remnants when out at the local
flea markets. Use pinking shears to cut into
placemats...they wipe clean in a jiffy!*

Cream of Tomato Soup

Bonnie Weber
West Palm Beach, FL

*Double this recipe for a great meal served with
grilled cheese sandwiches...yum!*

28-oz. can diced tomatoes   1 onion, chopped
1 c. chicken broth   1/8 t. baking soda
1/4 c. margarine   2 c. whipping cream

Combine the first 5 ingredients in a saucepan; cover and simmer for
one hour. Add cream to mixture just before serving and cook on low
until heated through. Makes 4 to 6 servings.

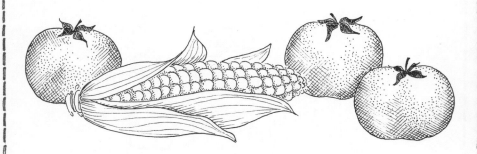

*Don't pass up bags of buttons found at tag sales. Use
them to dress up picture frames, bulletin boards,
lampshades, gift tags or flower pots...what fun!*

Savory Vegetable Soup

Natasha Roe
Sebring, FL

Chock full of vegetables, cheese and beef...this recipe is one
that will quickly become a part of your recipe file.

3/4 c. onion, chopped
3/4 c. carrots, shredded
3/4 c. celery, diced
1 t. dried basil
3 T. butter
1/4 c. all-purpose flour
3 c. chicken broth

4 c. potatoes, peeled and cubed
1 lb. ground beef, browned
8-oz. pkg. pasteurized process
    cheese spread, cubed
1-1/2 c. milk
salt and pepper to taste
1/4 c. sour cream

In a saucepan, sauté onion, carrots, celery and basil in butter for
5 minutes; stir in flour, broth, potatoes and beef. Cover; simmer for
15 minutes until potatoes are tender. Add cheese, milk, salt and
pepper; cook until cheese is melted. Remove from heat and blend in
sour cream. Serves 4 to 6.

Having friends over for a
Soup Supper? Create clever
placecards in no time.
Place a miniature
pumpkin in a candy
corn-filled ramekin. Slip
copper wire that's been
curled around a pencil
over the pumpkin stem
and then tuck in
the placecard.

Homemade Italian Bread

Susan Wagner
Humboldt, TN

This bread dough can be shaped into traditional loaves or rounds...either way, it's tasty with any meal.

2 pkgs. active dry yeast
3 c. warm water
3 T. oil
3 eggs

1 T. salt
1-1/4 c. sugar
10 to 11 c. plus 2 T. all-purpose
    flour

Dissolve yeast in warm water; set aside. In a large mixing bowl, combine oil, eggs, salt and sugar; stir in yeast mixture and gradually add 10 to 11 cups flour. Knead dough for 10 minutes. Place dough in an oiled bowl; cover and let rise in a warm place until double in bulk. Punch down and let rise again until almost double. Cut dough into 8 equal portions; cover and let rest 10 minutes. Flatten dough, pressing out all air and form into 8 oblong loaves. Place loaves on greased and floured baking sheets; cover and let rise 50 minutes. Sprinkle remaining flour on top of loaves; bake at 350 degrees for 30 to 35 minutes. Makes 8 loaves.

That first lock of hair, a treasured picture or a handwritten recipe card should be kept someplace special. Tucked inside a vellum envelope, they can still be seen and then easily slipped inside a memory book for safe keeping.

bountiful
SIDES
&
SALADS

Heavenly Potatoes

Sharon Spadaro
Houston, PA

You make these the night before...what a time saver!

6 potatoes, boiled, peeled
   and grated
2 pts. whipping cream, divided

onion salt to taste
pepper to taste

Layer half the potatoes in a lightly greased 13"x9" glass baking dish; pour one pint of whipping cream over top. Sprinkle with onion salt and pepper; repeat layers. Cover; refrigerate overnight. Bake at 350 degrees for one hour. Serves 8 to 10.

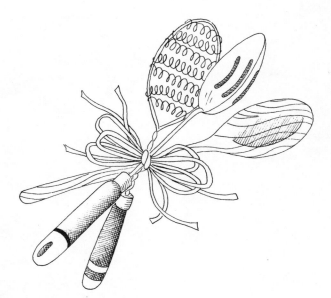

For a splash of color on a buffet table, line up Grandma's Fiestaware® pitchers filled with perky blossoms!

Baked Corn

Vivian Bowers
Shippensburg, PA

You can't go wrong with this...it's always popular.

2 c. creamed corn
1 c. evaporated milk
1 c. sugar

3 T. cornstarch
2 eggs
salt and pepper to taste

Mix all ingredients together; pour into a lightly greased 1-1/2 quart baking dish. Bake at 350 degrees for one hour. Serves 2 to 4.

BBQ Green Beans

Barbara Marschang
West Melbourne, FL

Try using different flavors of barbecue sauce...sweet, hickory or honey. They'll all give these beans their own special flavor.

6 slices bacon
1/2 c. onion, chopped
1 c. catsup
1 c. brown sugar, packed

2 T. barbecue sauce
3 14-1/2 oz. cans French-style
    green beans

Heat bacon and onion in a skillet; crisply cook bacon and sauté onion until soft. In a mixing bowl, combine catsup, sugar and barbecue sauce; add green beans, bacon and onion. Pour into a greased 2-quart baking dish; bake at 250 degrees for 2-1/2 hours. Serves 6.

Cucumber & Tomato Salad

Dianne Gregory
Sheridan, AR

The end of summer, when fresh garden tomatoes are nearly falling off the vine, is the perfect time for this salad.

2 cucumbers	3/4 t. salt
1 tomato	1/8 t. pepper
1/3 c. oil	1 green pepper, chopped
3 T. sugar	1 red onion, chopped
3 T. red wine vinegar	

Cut cucumbers and tomato in half; remove seeds and chop. In a large bowl, stir together oil, sugar, vinegar, salt and pepper; add all vegetables. Toss well to coat. Cover; chill for 3 hours. Makes about 2 cups.

If a rainy day is keeping the kids inside, collect goodies for puppet making. Spread craft sticks, scissors, glue, paper, stickers, markers, felt and buttons on the table and when they're done, they can put on a puppet show!

Sunflower Broccoli Slaw

Valerie Parrish
Beloit, WI

Crunchy and full of great flavor!

16-oz. pkg. broccoli slaw mix
2 bunches green onions,
   chopped
2 3-oz. pkgs. ramen noodles
   with seasoning packet,
   uncooked

1/3 c. white vinegar
1/2 c. sugar
1 c. oil
1/2 c. sunflower seeds
1/2 c. slivered almonds

Mix together broccoli slaw and onions. Break ramen noodles and toss with broccoli slaw mix; set aside. Combine ramen noodle seasoning, vinegar, sugar and oil; pour over slaw. Let stand at least 2 hours. Just before serving stir in sunflower seeds and almonds. Serves 4 to 6.

Hollowed-out peppers become fun salad bowls!
Whether it's a crispy green salad or more of a meal
made from chicken, tuna or egg salad, they're just the
right size and add a splash of color to the table.

Grandma's Sausage & Beans

Jody Gumber
Wooster, OH

My grandmother's recipe actually says, "Throw the whole mess together and cook for 15 to 20 minutes or as long as you want to!"

3 T. butter
1-1/2 lb. Polish sausage, cut
   into 1-1/2 inch slices
1-1/2 c. celery, sliced
3/4 c. green pepper, chopped

1/2 c. onion, chopped
1/8 t. garlic, chopped
16-oz. can pork & beans
15-oz. can chili beans
17-oz. can lima beans

Melt butter in a skillet; add sausage, celery, green pepper and onion, cooking until brown. Add remaining ingredients; cook for 15 to 20 minutes. Serves 6 to 8.

Remember those enameled lawn chairs that Grandma always had? Slightly springy and soothing as a rocker, they seemed made for relaxing in on a hot summer day. They're still available at flea markets or garage sales, so don't pass them up! A fresh coat of paint and it feels like 1950 all over again.

Spinach-Rice Bake

Nancy Rubeck
Raymond, OH

A simple way to prepare a side dish for any potluck or carry-in.

2 10-oz. pkgs. frozen, chopped
   spinach, cooked and drained
2 c. prepared rice
2 c. shredded Cheddar cheese
4 eggs, beaten
2/3 c. milk

1/4 c. butter, softened
1/4 c. onion, chopped
2 t. salt
1 t. Worcestershire sauce
1 t. dried thyme

Combine all ingredients in a large mixing bowl; stir well. Pour mixture into a greased 13"x9" baking pan. Cover and bake at 350 degrees for 20 minutes. Uncover and continue baking for 5 additional minutes until set. Serves 12 to 16.

There's no place like Grandma's

*On days when warmth is the most important
need of the human heart, the kitchen
is the place you can find it.*
-E.B. White

Pickled Egg & Red Beet Salad

Kristie Rigo
Friedens, PA

*My Grandma Beal would always make this salad and serve it on
pretty little plates to make us feel special...grandmas
always know how to make you feel special!*

2 14-1/2 oz. cans sliced red
   beets, juice reserved
1 c. water
2 t. vinegar, divided

2 T. sugar, divided
8 eggs, hard-boiled and peeled
1 head lettuce, torn

Combine, beets, water, vinegar, sugar and hard-boiled eggs in a bowl;
mix thoroughly. Cover; refrigerate for 24 hours until eggs are pink in
color. Cover individual serving plates with lettuce leaves. Cut eggs into
slices; arrange beets and egg on top of lettuce. Drizzle with dressing.
Serves 8.

Dressing:

3/4 c. mayonnaise
1/4 c. milk
1 T. sugar

1 t. vinegar
salt and pepper to taste
1 to 2 t. red beet juice

Mix all ingredients together in a jar with a lid; secure
lid and shake to blend thoroughly.

*Always tear lettuce into
bite-size pieces...a knife
can turn the edges brown!*

Curly Noodle Salad

Helen Baker
Fargo, ND

This pasta salad is a cinch to make during a busy week.

1 c. rotini noodles, uncooked
1/2 c. cucumber, peeled
   and sliced
1/4 c. onion, sliced
6 T. sugar
1/4 c. water

3 T. vinegar
3/4 t. mustard
3/4 t. dried parsley
1/4 t. pepper
1/4 t. salt
1/8 t. garlic salt

Cook noodles until tender; drain and rinse with cold water. Combine noodles, cucumber and onion in a large bowl; set aside. Mix together remaining ingredients in a jar with a lid; secure lid and shake well. Pour over noodle mixture; toss to coat. Cover and refrigerate for one hour. Makes about 2 servings.

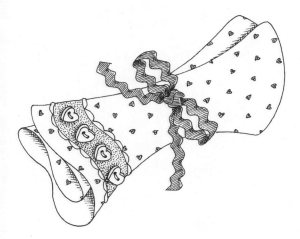

When a salad calls for noodles, there's so many shapes to choose from, why not experiment? Try using corkscrew, shell, bow tie and tricolor noodles just for fun!

Classic Rice Pilaf

Lisa Colombo
Appleton, WI

Try adding turkey, chicken or mushrooms for a whole new taste.

1 c. extra-fine egg noodles,
   uncooked
1/4 c. butter

1 c. instant long-grain rice,
   uncooked
2-1/4 c. chicken broth
salt to taste

In a saucepan, brown noodles in butter. Stir in rice. In a separate saucepan, bring chicken broth to a boil; add to noodles. Cover; simmer for 30 minutes. Sprinkle with salt. Serves 2 to 3.

Need a gift that's ready in no time? Tuck the dry
ingredients for Classic Rice Pilaf in a
vintage canning jar, tie on a recipe card
and share with a friend...so easy!

Bunk House Beans

Sheila Neal
Muscatine, IA

*My husband and his firefighter coworkers often enjoy
making (and eating!) this dish at the fire station.*

1 lb. ground beef
1/2 c. onion, chopped
15-oz. can butter beans
15-1/2 oz. can kidney beans
16-oz. can pork & beans

1 c. catsup
3/4 c. brown sugar, packed
1 t. dry mustard
1 T. vinegar

Brown beef and onion in a large skillet; drain. Combine all ingredients
in a bowl, mixing to combine. Place mixture in a greased
13"x9" baking pan. Bake at 350 degrees for one hour. Serves 6 to 8.

*Antique postcards make the prettiest pictures when
matted and framed. Since they're small, try
grouping three together in one frame...so sweet!*

Strawberry & Romaine Salad

Deidra Finney
Bakersfield, CA

So refreshing! Try it with your own dressing or the
Banana-Poppy Seed Dressing below.

2 c. romaine lettuce, torn   2 T. red onion, chopped
3/4 c. strawberries, sliced

Toss lettuce, strawberries and onion together. Serves one to 2.

Banana-Poppy Seed Dressing

Bridget Willard
Cedar Point, IL

Fruity cream-style dressing with a little tartness.

1 banana, mashed   1 T. lemon juice
1 c. sour cream   1 t. dry mustard
1/4 c. sugar   3/4 t. salt
1 T. poppy seed

Mix all ingredients together; chill for 30 minutes. Makes about 3 cups.

Make color copies of pretty vintage aprons for
one-of-a-kind scrapbook paper!

Crunchy Broccoli Salad

Judy Borecky
Escondido, CA

*There's so many variations on this tasty salad. Try tossing in
cauliflower, Cheddar cheese or raisins, too.*

1 bunch seedless green grapes,
   halved
1 bunch seedless red grapes,
   halved
1 bunch broccoli, finely chopped
1 red onion, chopped

8-oz. can sliced water chestnuts,
   drained
1/2 c. bacon, crisply cooked
   and crumbled
Garnish: sesame seed

Mix all ingredients together, except sesame seed, in a large mixing
bowl; toss well with dressing. Top with sesame seed just before
serving. Makes about 4 servings.

Dressing:

1 c. mayonnaise
1/2 c. sugar

3 T. cider vinegar

Whisk all ingredients together.

Golden Carrot Bake

Nancy Hauer
Rifle, CO

Tender carrots and cheese topped with a golden crumb crust.

8 to 10 carrots, sliced
1/2 c. margarine, divided

16-oz. pkg. pasteurized process
cheese spread, cubed
8 saltine crackers, crumbled

Steam carrots until crisp-tender; drain any liquid. In a saucepan, melt 3 tablespoons margarine and cheese; stir in carrots. Melt remaining margarine in a skillet; mix in cracker crumbs. Stir until golden. Place carrot mixture in a greased 2-quart baking dish; top with cracker mixture. Bake at 375 degrees for 15 to 20 minutes. Serves 4 to 6.

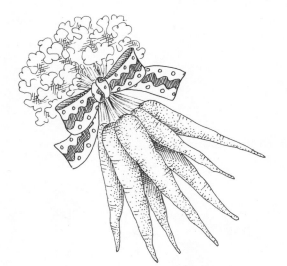

Traveling to a potluck or visiting a friend?
Keep side dishes warm by wrapping the baking dish
in aluminum foil, then covering it
with sheets of newspaper.

Easy Scalloped Potatoes

Renee Johnson
Smithville, TN

Buttery and oh-so simple to make.

2 t. butter
2 t. all-purpose flour
3/4 t. salt

1-3/4 c. milk
5 c. potatoes, peeled and sliced

Melt butter in a saucepan; whisk in flour and salt. Add milk, stirring constantly until sauce boils. Add potatoes, heating until potatoes are tender. Pour into a greased 13"x9" baking pan. Cover and bake at 350 degrees for 30 minutes. Serves 6 to 8.

Don't toss hand-me-downs that are less than perfect...quilt squares can be framed, popcorn-chenille bedspreads can be sized down into cozy throws and old tablecloths can be recycled into pillows.

Sweet & Sour Deviled Eggs

Karen Hazelett
Fort Wayne, IN

*Every family seems to have their own special recipe when
it comes to making deviled eggs. But try this sweet
and slightly tart recipe...we think you'll like it!*

12 eggs, hard-boiled and peeled
1 bunch green onions, diced
1/3 c. plus 1 T. mayonnaise
5 t. sugar
5 t. cider vinegar

1 t. mustard
1/2 t. salt
1/4 t. pepper
1/2 t. paprika
Garnish: fresh parsley, chopped

Slice eggs in half lengthwise, remove yolk and set whites aside. In a
small bowl, mash yolks with a fork. Add onions, mayonnaise, sugar,
vinegar, mustard, salt and pepper. Fill each egg white with
1/2 tablespoon mixture using a spoon or pastry bag. Sprinkle paprika
over top. Garnish with parsley. Makes 2 dozen.

*Save flowers from special
occasions and let them dry
naturally. Tucked in a
vase or made into
potpourri, they will be a
sweet reminder of
a wedding bouquet,
Mother's Day corsage
or walk through
grandma's garden.*

Green Pea Salad

Carol Murphy
La Grande, OR

A sure way to get the kids to eat their vegetables!

4 slices bacon, crisply cooked
  and crumbled
3 green onions, sliced
1 stalk celery, diced
10-oz. pkg. frozen peas, thawed

1/4 c. mayonnaise
1/4 c. sour cream
1/4 t. salt
1/8 t. pepper

Combine all ingredients together in a mixing bowl. Chill before serving. Serves 6.

Summertime Egg Salad

Janet Isom
Paragould, AR

Served on a bed of crisp, shredded lettuce, this makes a terrific light lunch anytime.

3-oz. pkg. cream cheese,
  softened
1/4 c. mayonnaise
3/4 t. dill weed
6 eggs, hard-boiled, peeled
  and chopped

1/4 c. sliced black olives
2 T. onion, chopped
1/4 c. celery, chopped
1/2 t. salt

Mix all ingredients together; chill in refrigerator before serving. Makes about 4 servings.

To get a little extra zing, add a squeeze of lemon or lime to any salad!

Old-Fashioned Potato Salad

Tina Langseth
Springfield, MN

You can also make this with new red potatoes and tiny, just-shelled peas.

1 c. mayonnaise-type salad
    dressing
2/3 c. sugar
1 t. mustard
1 T. vinegar
1 onion, chopped

1 stalk celery, chopped
2 eggs, hard-boiled, peeled
    and chopped
8 potatoes, peeled, boiled
    and cubed
salt and pepper to taste

Mix together salad dressing, sugar, mustard and vinegar. Stir in onion, celery, eggs and cooled potatoes. Salt and pepper to taste. Serves 6 to 8.

Kids big and small will love tortilla bowls filled with a crisp, crunchy salad! Spray one side of a tortilla and the inside of an oven-safe bowl with non-stick vegetable spray. Place the tortilla in the bowl, oiled side up, and bake at 350 degrees for 15 minutes or until golden; let cool before filling.

Grandpa's Okra

Tresha Hoover
Salina, KS

As a little girl growing up in Kansas, I remember my grandfather had the most beautiful garden in town! He had a huge lot next to his house and filled it with everything you could imagine. He truly enjoyed providing the entire neighborhood with fresh veggies all summer.

1 c. cornmeal
1/2 t. salt
1/2 t. pepper
1 egg
1 T. milk

6 c. okra, sliced
1 lb. bacon, cut into
   one-inch strips
2 c. new potatoes, peeled
   and quartered

Mix together cornmeal, salt and pepper; set aside. In a separate bowl, beat egg with milk until smooth. Dip okra into egg mixture, draining excess off. Then, dip each okra slice into cornmeal mixture and coat well. Combine okra, bacon and potatoes in a skillet; cook until golden. Serves 4 to 6.

Disposable cameras are great for a family reunion! Lightweight and simple to use, set them out where they're easily picked up to capture all the silly and heartfelt moments.

Onion-Potato Gratin

Kathy Unruh
Fresno, CA

*Serve these with a tender roast pork for a very special
"meat & potatoes" dinner.*

5 potatoes, peeled and sliced
2 T. olive oil, divided
1 onion, chopped
1 c. whipping cream

1 t. fresh rosemary, minced
salt and pepper to taste
3/4 c. fontina cheese, grated and
  divided

Place sliced potatoes in a mixing bowl, cover with water and set aside.
Heat one tablespoon olive oil in a small skillet until smoking hot; add
onion. Cook until onion has caramelized to a dark brown color, about
5 minutes; set aside to cool. Mix together cream, rosemary, salt and
pepper; set aside. Heat the remaining olive oil in a 2-quart oven-safe
baking dish; add enough potatoes to cover the bottom. Cook until
browned; remove from heat. Sprinkle with half onion and half cheese;
drizzle with half cream mixture. Add a layer of uncooked potatoes,
remaining onion and cheese; drizzle with remaining cream. Top with
any remaining potatoes. Bake at 425 degrees for 25 to 35 minutes;
cool 5 minutes. Flip over onto a plate. Serves 6.

*A discarded window shutter makes a very clever
serving tray...crumbs can just be brushed
through the slats!*

Fresh Basil & Tomato Salad

Brenda Brown
Keller, TX

Using hollowed-out peppers as serving bowls makes clean up a snap!

4 c. tomatoes, chopped
2 bunches green onions,
    chopped
1 c. fresh basil, chopped
1/2 T. olive oil

1/2 t. salt
1 c. balsamic vinegar
1/2 t. pepper
3 yellow peppers, halved and
    seeded

Mix together tomatoes, onions and basil; set aside. Whisk together olive oil, salt, vinegar and pepper; pour over tomato mixture. Let mixture stand at room temperature for 2 hours so flavors can blend. Spoon into pepper halves before serving. Serves 6.

When making homemade croutons, add a little zip with a sprinkle of Parmesan cheese, dried herbs, paprika or chili powder.

Old-Fashioned Tomato Bake

Pamela Lester
Helena, OH

This has been a family favorite for years and whenever we have guests visiting for the holidays, this is the dish they rave about.

2 c. brown sugar, packed
1/2 c. water
21-oz. can tomato purée

8 slices bread, crusts trimmed
1 c. butter, melted

In a saucepan, combine sugar, water and tomato purée; bring to a boil for 5 minutes. Cube bread and place in a lightly greased 2-quart baking dish; drizzle butter over top. Pour purée mixture over bread; bake at 350 degrees for 30 minutes. Makes 4 to 6 servings.

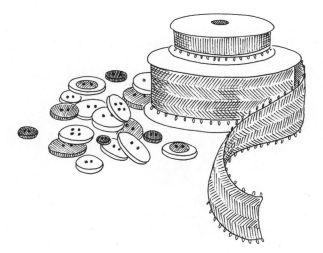

Make notecards really special...sepia-toned photos, button cards, silk ribbons or color copies of vintage wallpaper all make one-of-a-kind cards anyone will cherish.

Brown Sugar Sweet Potatoes

Elizabeth Roundtree
Petersburg, AK

Every Thanksgiving Gramma Izzy made these sweet potatoes, but the year she shared the recipe with me and it was my turn to bring them, I worried if I would measure up. Would they be just like Gramma's? Well, I passed the test…they're still a Roundtree family favorite!

8 sweet potatoes, peeled and
   cubed
1 c. corn syrup

1/2 c. butter
2 c. brown sugar, packed

Boil potatoes until just tender. Drain and place in an electric skillet; set aside. In a saucepan, combine corn syrup, butter and brown sugar. Heat until melted, then bring to a boil for 2 to 3 minutes. Pour sauce over potatoes. Cover and simmer until heated through. Serves 6 to 8.

Don't pass up a trellis or stepladder at the next flea market…use them to decorate in unusual ways. A trellis can be a great quilt rack, and a step ladder is an oh-so-handy nightstand!

Saucy Ham & Beans

Beverly Smith
Malin, OR

*Long cooking brings out the most delicious flavor and fills
the house with an incredible aroma.*

2 30-oz. cans pork & beans
1 onion, chopped
1/2 c. green pepper, chopped
1/8 t. garlic powder
2/3 c. brown sugar, packed

1 c. catsup
2 t. chili powder
2 T. Worcestershire sauce
1 c. chopped, cooked ham
Optional: 1 t. liquid smoke

Combine all ingredients; pour into an ungreased 13"x9" baking pan.
Bake at 325 degrees for 2 to 3 hours until sauce is thickened. Serves
8 to 10.

*Make the family tree more interesting! Hang color
copies of photos, tied with ribbon, on a white-washed
branch that's been tucked in a sap bucket. Show the
kids Aunt Lucille or Uncle Bob...it will make
sharing family stories much more fun.*

7-Layer Salad

Nancy Willis
Farmington Hills, MI

Be sure to serve this in a glass dish...the colors are beautiful.

1 head lettuce, chopped
1 lb. baby spinach, chopped
1 lb. bacon, crisply cooked
   and crumbled
10-oz. pkg. frozen peas, thawed
1 bunch green onions, chopped

8 eggs, hard-boiled, peeled
   and chopped
2 c. sour cream
2 c. mayonnaise
1-oz. pkg. ranch salad
   dressing mix

Layer lettuce, spinach, bacon, peas, onions and eggs in a 13"x9" dish. Mix together sour cream, mayonnaise and salad dressing mix; spread over salad. Serves 6 to 8.

Try making homemade salad dressings. The taste is unbeatable and most recipes are really short, like this one for Tangy Green Onion Dressing: Blend 1/3 cup mayonnaise, 1/4 cup sour cream, 1 tablespoon milk, 1 teaspoon lemon juice and 2 finely chopped green onions. How easy!

Orangy Baked Sweet Potatoes

Delinda Blakney
Bridgeview, IL

These have a wonderful sweet, brown sugar coating.

4 sweet potatoes
salt water
2 T. brown sugar, packed

1 T. butter
1 orange, peeled and halved

Cook sweet potatoes in salt water until tender; drain, peel and halve each potato. Place potatoes in a lightly greased 2-quart baking dish. In a separate bowl, mix together brown sugar and butter and juice of one orange half; pour over potatoes. Cut remaining orange half in slices; lay slices over potatoes; bake at 350 degrees for 20 to 30 minutes. Serves 6 to 8.

For nostalgic lanterns that glow like fireflies, use milk glass jelly jars. Wrap a piece of 14-gauge wire securely around the neck of each jar and then bring the ends up and twist together to make a loop.

4-Bean Bake

Lorraine Roethlisberger
Shepherd, MI

A blend of beans, brown sugar and molasses combine to make this dish anything but ordinary.

1/2 lb. ground beef
1 onion, chopped
1 lb. bacon, crisply cooked
    and crumbled
1/2 c. brown sugar, packed
1/2 c. sugar
1/4 c. catsup
1/4 c. barbecue sauce
2 t. mustard
2 t. molasses
1/2 t. chili powder

1 t. pepper
1/2 t. salt
16-oz. can butter beans,
    drained
16-oz. can kidney beans,
    drained
31-oz. can pork & beans,
    drained
16-oz. can Great Northern
    beans, drained

Brown beef and onion in a large skillet; drain well. Combine all ingredients in a 6-quart slow cooker. Cook on high for one hour. Reduce temperature to low and cook for 3 additional hours. Makes 12 to 15 servings.

Charm bracelets, whether handed down or new, are a wonderful way to welcome a baby. Although it won't be worn for many years, it's like going on a treasure hunt to fill it for "someday."

Country-Style Green Tomatoes

Billie Smith
Rock View, WV

A tried & true recipe.

2 green tomatoes
1 c. cornmeal

bacon drippings for frying
salt and pepper to taste

Slice each tomato 1/4-inch thick. Roll each slice in cornmeal to coat. Fry tomatoes in bacon drippings until golden and crisp. Sprinkle with salt and pepper. Serves 2 to 3.

Fried Dill Pickles

Sheila Williams
Mayodan, NC

This county fair recipe is one everybody needs!

1 egg, beaten
1 c. milk
1 T. Worcestershire sauce
3-1/2 c. plus 1 T. all-purpose
   flour, divided

6 drops hot pepper sauce
3/4 t. salt
3/4 t. pepper
1 qt. dill pickles, sliced
oil for deep frying

Combine egg, milk, Worcestershire sauce, one tablespoon flour and hot sauce; set aside. Mix together salt, pepper and remaining flour. Dip pickles in milk mixture, then in flour mixture. Deep fry in 350-degree oil until pickles are golden; drain. Serves 4 to 6.

Vintage canisters in blue, red, yellow and lime are not only terrific for corralling clutter, they add festive color wherever they're sitting!

Hushpuppies

*Jennifer Dartlon
Oak Grove, LA*

It's said that the name hushpuppy came about when an old Creole cook was cooking fish outdoors and his dogs began to howl in anticipation of a chance to taste some food. However the cook tossed a few deep fried corn fritters to the dogs and yelled, "Hush, puppies!" and the name stuck.

1 c. cornmeal	14-3/4 oz. can creamed corn
1 c. self-rising flour	1 t. sugar
1 t. salt	1 onion, chopped
1 t. pepper	garlic salt to taste
1 t. baking powder	oil for deep frying
1 egg	

Combine all ingredients except oil in a large mixing bowl. Drop batter by tablespoonfuls into 365-degree oil; cook hushpuppies, 5 to 6 at a time, until golden. Remove from oil with a slotted spoon and roll on paper towels to briefly drain. Makes about one dozen.

This summer keep a gardening scrapbook...what fun to look back on! Tuck in pictures of the kids gardening with Grandma, and don't forget to add recipes for favorite garden-fresh delights!

Marshmallow Ambrosia

Sue Utley
Papillion, NE

*No family reunion is complete unless someone brings
Marshmallow Ambrosia!*

2 c. mini marshmallows
1 banana, sliced
8-oz. can pineapple chunks,
   drained

1 c. orange sections
1/2 c. sour cream
1 c. flaked coconut

Combine all ingredients except coconut; mix lightly. Refrigerate 2 to
3 hours until chilled. Stir in coconut just before serving. Serves 6.

Very Cherry Salad

Carol Burns
Gooseberry Patch

Choose this recipe when looking for a quick, fruity side dish.

21-oz. can cherry pie filling
15-1/4 oz. can fruit cocktail,
   drained

3 bananas, sliced

Mix together all ingredients in a large bowl. Chill 2 to 3 hours before
serving. Makes 8 to 10 servings.

Frosty Strawberry Salad

Crystal Andersen
Grain Valley, MO

Cool and creamy...almost like old-fashioned rice pudding.

3 c. cold water
1/2 c. instant rice, uncooked
1/2 t. salt
1/4 c. sugar

3-oz. pkg. strawberry gelatin
  mix
8-oz. can crushed pineapple
8-oz. container frozen whipped
  topping, thawed

Combine water, rice and salt in a saucepan; cover. Cook on high until steaming. Reduce heat; simmer 20 to 25 minutes. Remove from heat; add sugar and strawberry gelatin. Stir until dissolved; add undrained pineapple. Mix well; refrigerate until set. Fold in whipped topping. Makes 4 to 6 servings.

Check out craft stores for large 7-inch clothespins...they make such handy recipe card holders!

Baked Eggplant Italiano

*Caroline Kim
San Gabriel, CA*

*Don't believe it when someone says they don't like
eggplant...they've never tried this!*

4 eggplants, halved
1 t. salt
1 t. pepper
6 T. olive oil, divided
4 roma tomatoes, diced

1 t. dried basil
1 t. dried oregano
Garnish: grated Parmesan
  cheese

Place eggplant halves in an ungreased 13"x9" baking pan cut-side up.
Sprinkle each eggplant half with salt, pepper and 1/2 tablespoon of
olive oil; score each half. Bake at 375 degrees for 30 minutes. Heat
remaining olive oil in a skillet; add tomatoes, basil and oregano.
Simmer for 15 minutes; spoon over eggplants. Top with cheese.
Serves 8.

Clever reunion
name tags...rubber
stamp names on
lengths of
light-colored
ribbon and glue a
button at the
top. Attach a
pin-back behind
the button with hot
glue and it's done!

Hearty Skillet Cabbage

Sherry Collins
Van Lear, KY

*Cooked just until tender and topped with crispy bacon,
this side is terrific with pork chops or ham.*

4 slices bacon
1 c. onion, diced
1-lb. head cabbage, shredded

1/4 c. water
1 t. salt
1/4 t. pepper

Fry bacon in a large skillet; add onion to sauté for 3 minutes. Add remaining ingredients, cover and bring to a boil. Simmer about 12 minutes. Uncover and continue stirring until most of the liquid is absorbed. Serves 4 to 6.

A decoupaged suitcase is a nifty way to store favorite treasures. Paint it a cheery color on the outside and line the inside with pretty giftwrap; it'll easily stay in place with spray adhesive. Decoupage copies of kids' artwork, letters from friends or newspaper clippings and place on the outside, while tucking the originals safely inside.

Cornbread Salad

Jamie Cox
Broken Arrow, OK

This old-fashioned salad is really very good!

3 8-1/2 oz. pkgs.
   cornbread mix
6 to 8 radishes, thinly sliced

1 green pepper, chopped
1 bunch green onions, chopped
3 tomatoes, chopped

Prepare cornbread as directed on package. Allow to cool, then crumble bread in a large bowl. Add all vegetables. Pour dressing over top 15 minutes before serving, tossing to coat. Serves 6 to 8.

Dressing:

1 c. cucumber dressing
3/4 c. mayonnaise-type salad
   dressing

3 T. mustard

Blend together all ingredients.

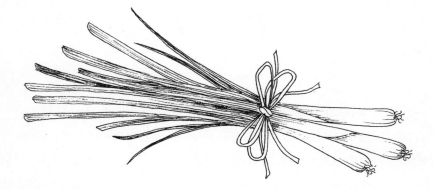

Serve meals on your very best china and linens...what are you saving them for?

The Best Tossed Garden Salad

Theone Neel
Bastian, VA

*Fill vintage milk bottles with a variety of salad dressings,
and then tuck them in a milk carrier...so clever!*

1 head lettuce, torn
1 head cabbage, shredded
6 green onions, sliced
1 green pepper, chopped
3 tomatoes, chopped

1 to 2 cucumbers, peeled
   and chopped
1 c. celery, chopped
1 c. radishes, sliced
1/2 c. carrots, grated

Combine ingredients in a large mixing bowl; toss with dressing before
serving. Serves 4 to 6.

Dressing:

1 c. mayonnaise
1/2 c. sugar
1/4 c. vinegar

1 to 2 t. mustard
salt and pepper to taste

Combine all ingredients; mix well.

Nestle 2 sizes of enamelware bowls together. Fill the bottom one with crushed ice and add a crispy salad to the top bowl...keeps salads cool in hot weather!

Delicious Vegetable Medley

Vickie

*For a colorful salad that can be made a couple hours before dinner,
try this great combination of garden vegetables.*

1 c. broccoli flowerets
1 c. cucumber, sliced
1 yellow pepper, sliced
1 c. cherry tomatoes, halved

3/4 c. carrots, sliced
2 T. fresh parsley, chopped
1/2 c. Italian dressing
1 T. Dijon mustard

Combine first 6 ingredients in a large bowl. Mix together dressing and
mustard in a separate bowl; pour over vegetables. Cover and
refrigerate 2 hours to marinate. Serves 8.

Dilly New Potatoes

Nita Pilkington
Reeds Spring, MO

Ready in less than 20 minutes!

1/4 c. oil
1 lb. new redskin potatoes,
   halved

3 T. rice vinegar
3 T. fresh dill, minced
salt and pepper to taste

Heat oil in a heavy skillet; add potatoes. Sauté until lightly golden and
tender, about 15 minutes. Add vinegar; cook 3 to 4 minutes. Sprinkle
with dill, salt and pepper. Serves 4.

Slow-Cooker Beans

*Darcy Anders
Hendersonville, NC*

*Tossing everything in the slow cooker
means more time with the family!*

1 lb. ground beef
1 onion, chopped
4 to 6 slices bacon, crisply
    cooked and crumbled
2 T. oil
1 c. catsup

1 T. Worcestershire sauce
1 t. cider vinegar
1 t. mustard
1 t. salt
1/3 c. brown sugar, packed
2 16-oz. cans pork & beans

Brown beef and onion; set aside. Mix together bacon, oil, catsup,
Worcestershire sauce, vinegar, mustard, salt and brown sugar; add to
beef. Stir in beans. Pour mixture into a slow cooker; heat on high for
one hour. Serves 6 to 8.

*Make family
gatherings full of
fun...a pie-eating
contest, watermelon
roll, potato sack and
3-legged race will
make memories that
last a lifetime!*

Fluffy Pineapple Salad

Peggy Forrest
Shelbyville, IN

The kids will love this…it's a must-have at any get-together!

1/2 c. sugar	20-oz. can pineapple chunks,
3 T. cornstarch	juice reserved
1/8 t. salt	1 t. butter
1 egg, beaten	2 c. mini marshmallows

In a saucepan, mix sugar, cornstarch and salt together; add egg and one cup reserved pineapple juice. Cook until mixture thickens; stir in butter. Let cool; add pineapple and marshmallows. Serves 2 to 3.

Long before electronic games, kids played with
pocket puzzles. They had to tilt, nudge and wiggle
puzzle pieces into place…get the eyeglasses
on the man or the dog's bones on the platter.
Still found at flea markets, they're as much fun
today as when they were made!

FAMILY
STYLE
Main
dishes

Savory Chicken Pies

Carrie Smith
Xenia, OH

*Chunks of chicken in rich broth, topped with a flaky
crust...comfort food doesn't get any better than this.*

4 T. butter
1-1/3 c. all-purpose flour,
   divided
3/4 t. salt, divided
1/8 t. pepper
1-3/4 c. chicken broth
2/3 c. milk
2 c. chicken, cooked and cubed

10-oz. pkg. frozen peas
1/2 lb. ground sausage,
   browned
1 t. celery seed
1/2 t. paprika
1/3 c. shortening
2 T. water

Melt butter in a saucepan; blend in 1/3 cup flour, 1/4 teaspoon salt
and pepper. Add broth and milk, stirring until thickened. Cook for one
additional minute. Add chicken, peas and sausage; heat through.
Divide evenly among 6, one-cup baking dishes; set aside. Mix
together remaining flour, celery seed, remaining salt and paprika; cut
in shortening. Sprinkle with water and mix with a fork. Press dough
into a ball; roll out to 1/8-inch thickness on a floured surface. Cut into
6 circles the size of each dish; place one on top of each, crimping
edges to seal. Bake at 425 degrees for 25 to 30 minutes. Serves 6.

Slow-Cooker Meat Loaf

Marie Blackman
Crown Point, IN

*A homestyle favorite when served with mashed potatoes
and green beans.*

1-1/2 lbs. ground beef
2 eggs
3/4 c. milk
1 onion, chopped
1 t. salt
1/4 t. pepper

3/4 c. bread crumbs
1/4 c. catsup
2 T. brown sugar, packed
1 t. dry mustard
1/4 t. nutmeg

Mix together beef, eggs, milk, onion, salt, pepper and bread crumbs; form mixture into a loaf and place in slow cooker. Cook on low 5 to 6 hours. Combine remaining ingredients; pour over meat. Cook on high 15 additional minutes. Serves 4 to 6.

Make a scrapbook cover that's as pretty as it is full of memories. Cut flower shapes from grandma's felt scraps and glue a button in the middle of each. "Plant" flowers on the cover using glue; let dry.

GRANDMA'S
MEMORIES

Grandaddy Hite's BBQ Chicken

Mary Nell Thomas
Newport News, VA

*This recipe is so dear to me because my dad cooked this BBQ for
more special occasions than I can remember. He's taught
3 generations how to prepare this tasty dish.*

4 3 to 4-lb. chickens	1 qt. vinegar
salt water	6-oz. bottle hot pepper sauce
1 lb. butter, melted	8-oz. can tomato sauce
1 c. sugar	pepper to taste

Soak chicken in salt water for one to 2 hours before cooking. Split
each chicken in half. Cook for an hour over a slow charcoal fire,
turning often to cook both sides. Combine remaining ingredients in a
large saucepan; bring to a boil. Continue cooking chicken for one
additional hour, basting with sauce every 10 to 15 minutes. Serves
16 to 20.

*A quick & easy centerpiece...fill a clear vase with
lots of colorful plastic buttons, add the flowers and
then water. The buttons hold the stems in place and
add a cheery look to any table!*

Crunchy Pecan Fish

Nancy Johnson
South Lake Tahoe, CA

Flaky fillets coated and then topped with pecans.

1 lb. catfish or whitefish fillets	1/4 t. pepper
1/4 c. bread crumbs	1/4 c. all-purpose flour
2 T. cornmeal	1/4 c. milk
2 T. grated Parmesan cheese	oil for frying
2 T. ground pecans	1/3 c. chopped pecans
1/4 t. salt	

Divide fish into 4 portions; set aside. In a bowl, mix together bread crumbs, cornmeal, Parmesan cheese, ground pecans, salt and pepper. Coat each piece of fish with flour, then dip each in milk. Coat evenly with crumb mixture. Heat oil in a skillet; add fish and fry 4 to 6 minutes on each side. Add chopped pecans to skillet; cook and stir an additional 2 minutes. Serves 4.

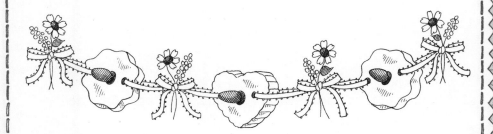

An old-fashioned fish fry is a terrific way to get together with friends & family. Usually held once a year in small towns, it has some of the best food around...crunchy fish, creamy cole slaw, homemade bread and a variety of desserts that can't be beat!

Quick & Easy Skillet Supper

Gloria Heather
Cincinnati, OH

My family loves this speedy dish...especially when I serve it with corn on the cob.

1-1/2 lbs. ground sausage
1 onion, chopped
1/4 t. pepper
1 t. dried marjoram
2 15-oz. cans chopped
   tomatoes

10-oz. pkg. frozen chopped
   spinach, thawed and drained
5 to 6 c. prepared rotini pasta
Garnish: grated Parmesan
   cheese

Brown sausage in a large skillet; drain. Add onion; sauté until tender. Stir in pepper, marjoram, tomatoes and spinach. Add pasta, stirring to combine. Sprinkle cheese over top. Serves 4 to 6.

Grandma's Big Roaster Dinner

Patti Angeles
Valley City, ND

Everyone in my family loves Grandma's recipe.

1 lb. ground beef
1 onion, chopped
1/4 c. instant rice, uncooked

10-3/4 oz. can tomato soup
1 c. hot water
1 head cabbage, shredded

Brown beef and onion in a large skillet; add rice, tomato soup and hot water; simmer 8 to 10 minutes. Layer cabbage in the bottom of a roaster; pour beef mixture over top. Cover and cook at 350 degrees for one hour. Serves 4 to 6.

Peace...that was the other name for home.
-Kathleen Norris

Homemade Pizza

Pam James
Gooseberry Patch

My grandmother would make this pizza for my slumber parties. I can still remember the surprise from my friends when the pizza was served. How we enjoyed sitting around the table eating pizza and drinking Coca-Cola from glass bottles!

1 T. sugar	1/4 c. warm water
3/4 t. salt	2-3/4 c. all-purpose flour
3 T. oil	2 8-oz. pkgs. shredded
1/2 c. milk, scalded	mozzarella cheese
1 pkg. active dry yeast	

Stir sugar, salt and oil into scalded milk; heat to lukewarm and set aside. In a separate bowl, dissolve yeast in warm water; add milk mixture and flour. Turn dough out onto a lightly floured surface; knead until smooth and elastic. Place dough in a greased bowl; spray dough with non-stick vegetable spray. Cover and let rise in a warm place for one hour or until double in bulk. Divide dough in half. Roll out each half to fit a 12" pizza pan, folding under 1/2 inch around edges. Bake at 425 degrees for 5 minutes. Remove from oven; top each pizza with sauce and cheese. Bake an additional 12 to 15 minutes or until crust is golden. Serves 12 to 15.

Sauce:

12-oz. can tomato paste	1 clove garlic, minced
1 t. salt	1/4 t. pepper
1/2 c. water	1/2 t. sugar
1/2 t. dried oregano	

Combine all ingredients. Bring to a boil over medium heat; simmer 10 minutes.

Granny's Baked Chicken

Dyane Adams-Snyder
San Diego, CA

Good when hot and even better later in salads or
sandwiches...if there's any left over!

3 to 4 lbs. chicken　　　　　　1/2 c. vinegar
1 c. butter　　　　　　　　　　salt and pepper to taste
3 T. Worcestershire sauce

Arrange chicken, skin-side up, in a lightly greased 13"x9" baking pan.
Heat butter, Worcestershire sauce and vinegar together in a saucepan
until butter is melted; pour over chicken. Salt and pepper to taste.
Cover and bake at 350 degrees for 2 to 2-1/2 hours, removing cover
for last 15 minutes. Serves 4 to 6.

When heading to a picnic, an enamelware pail is
ideal for toting bottles of root beer or cream soda.
Filled with crushed ice, it keeps the bottles chilled and
ready to enjoy after a family softball game!

Pork Chops with Apples & Stuffing

Kathy McLaren
Visalia, CA

Fuss is minimal for this terrific pork dish.

6 boneless pork chops
1 T. oil
6-oz. pkg. pork-flavored
    stuffing mix

21-oz. can apple pie filling with
    cinnamon

Brown pork chops in oil over medium-high heat. Prepare stuffing mix according to package directions; set aside. Spread pie filling in the bottom of a greased 13"x9" baking pan; place pork chops on top. Spoon stuffing mix over top; cover. Bake at 350 degrees for 35 minutes; uncover and bake and additional 10 minutes. Serves 6.

Fill an old copper boiler with water and float apple candles inside for a beautiful fall decoration. The candles are easy to make...just hollow out an apple and tuck a votive inside.

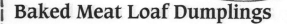

Baked Meat Loaf Dumplings

Tracy Quaglietti
Bellingham, MA

A yummy spin on traditional meat loaf.

2-1/4 c. all-purpose flour	3/4 c. shortening
1 t. salt	1/4 c. water

Sift together flour and salt in a mixing bowl; remove 1/3 cup mixture and set aside. Cut shortening into flour mixture to resemble coarse crumbs. Mix reserved 1/3 cup mixture with water to make a paste; add to crumb mixture to form a dough. Shape into a ball; turn onto a lightly floured surface and divide in half. Roll each half to 1/8-inch thickness; cut each into three, 6"x6" squares. Place 1/2 cup filling in the center of each square; bring edges together and seal. Place dumplings in a lightly greased jelly roll pan; bake at 400 degrees for one hour until golden. Serves 4 to 6.

Filling:

1 lb. ground beef	1/4 t. pepper
1/3 c. bread crumbs	1/3 c. catsup
2 T. onion, chopped	1 egg
1 t. salt	

Combine all ingredients, mixing well.

Best Beef Brisket

Lynda McCormick
Burkburnett, TX

Fork-tender and delicious.

1 t. garlic salt
1 t. garlic powder
1-3/4 t. kosher salt
2 t. pepper
2 T. Worcestershire sauce

5 to 6-lb. beef brisket, trimmed
1/3 c. sugar
1 c. barbecue sauce
1 c. Russian salad dressing

Combine first 5 ingredients; rub into beef. Tightly wrap beef in heavy aluminum foil; place in an ungreased 13"x9" baking pan. Cook at 300 degrees for 5 to 6 hours. Carefully remove foil from beef and discard. Place beef on a serving platter; set aside. Measure and reserve one cup of broth; discard any remaining. Slice brisket and return to baking pan. Mix together broth and remaining ingredients; pour over brisket slices. Bake, uncovered, at 325 degrees for one hour. Serves 6 to 8.

Make a nostalgic candle holder in no time. Invert a pretty stoneware bowl, center a smaller one on top and set a plump pillar candle inside...so simple!

Hamburger-Biscuit Pie

Amy Bradford
Emporia, KS

When my husband and I were first married, my in-laws gave me a cookbook of their family recipes...this is one of my husband's favorites.

1 lb. ground beef
1/2 c. onion, chopped
4-oz. can mushroom pieces, drained
3-oz. pkg. cream cheese
2 T. all-purpose flour
1/4 t. salt
1/8 t. pepper
1/8 t. garlic powder
10-oz. tube refrigerated biscuits
1 egg, beaten
3/4 c. cottage cheese
Garnish: paprika

Brown beef and onion in a large skillet; drain. Stir in mushrooms, cream cheese, flour, salt, pepper and garlic powder. Heat until cheese is melted. Arrange biscuits in an ungreased 9" round pan; press along bottom and sides to form a crust. Spoon beef mixture on top. Blend egg and cottage cheese together; spread over meat mixture. Sprinkle top with paprika. Bake at 350 degrees for 25 to 30 minutes. Serves 6 to 8.

Create a backyard hideaway anywhere with cast-off sections of picket fencing. Given a face lift with a coat of paint and hinges to keep sections together, it's portable to move around as needed!

Chicken-Lickin' Pork Chops

Marcie Shaffer
Westminster, MD

Serve this with baked sweet potatoes and buttered vegetables
for a hearty family dinner.

1 c. all-purpose flour
1 t. dry mustard
salt and pepper to taste
6 pork chops

2 T. oil
2 10-3/4 oz. cans chicken and
   rice soup

Place flour, mustard, salt and pepper in a plastic zipping bag; shake to
combine. Add pork chops to bag and shake to coat. Heat oil in large
skillet; add pork chops, browning on both sides. Pour soup into a slow
cooker; add pork chops. Cook on low for 8 to 10 hours. Serves 6.

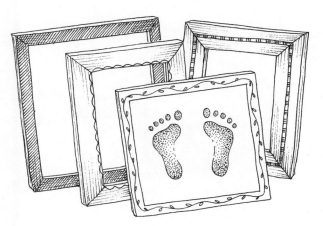

Create a family photo collage to capture favorite
memories. Fill a wall with single-photo frames of
best-loved moments and special occasions. A tiny
3-inch frame is the perfect size for holding copies of
baby's sweet footprints.

Zucchini Quiche

Barbara Faulkner
Greenwood, SC

No need to roll out pastry, the crust magically appears!

3 c. zucchini, thinly sliced
1 c. biscuit baking mix
1/2 c. onion, chopped
1/2 c. grated Parmesan cheese
2 T. dried parsley
1/2 t. salt

1/2 t. dried oregano
1/8 t. pepper
1/8 t. garlic powder
1/2 c. oil
4 eggs, slightly beaten

Combine all ingredients in a large mixing bowl; blend well. Pour into a greased 9" round baking pan. Bake at 350 degrees for 45 minutes or until lightly golden. Cut into wedges. Serves 4 to 6.

Use any favorite quiche recipe to make mini quiches.
Just pour ingredients into muffin tins and bake
until the centers are set...so simple!

Chicken Cordon Bleu

Jen Sell
Farmington, MN

A special dish I serve family & friends...it's delicious every time.

4 boneless, skinless
   chicken breasts
4 slices cooked ham
4 slices Swiss cheese
8 slices bacon
2 eggs

1/2 c. milk
1/2 c. all-purpose flour
3/4 c. bread crumbs
1/2 t. garlic powder
1 t. dried oregano
1/4 c. grated Parmesan cheese

Flatten chicken breasts between 2 pieces of wax paper until 1/4-inch thick. Top each piece with a slice of ham and cheese; roll up tightly. Wrap 2 slices of bacon around each bundle, securing with toothpicks. In a small bowl, beat eggs and milk together; set aside. Place flour in a separate bowl; set aside. In a third bowl, combine bread crumbs, garlic powder, oregano and Parmesan cheese. Dip each chicken bundle in egg mixture, then in flour. Dip in egg mixture again, and lastly in bread crumb mixture. Place on a greased baking sheet; bake at 350 degrees for 45 minutes. Serves 4.

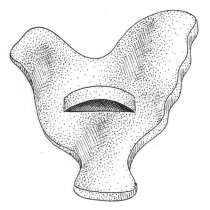

Make sweet memories...rediscover the wee world of dollhouses with a daughter or granddaughter.

Kentucky Hot Brown

Renee Brooks
Utica, KY

Tender turkey hidden under lots of bubbly cheese and bacon.

2 T. butter
2 T. all-purpose flour
salt and cayenne pepper to taste
1/4 t. curry powder
1 c. milk
3/4 c. shredded American
   cheese, divided

3/4 c. shredded sharp Cheddar
   cheese, divided
4 slices bread, toasted
4 slices turkey
8 slices bacon, slightly cooked

Melt butter in a saucepan; whisk in flour, salt, cayenne pepper and curry. Stir until bubbly and remove from heat. Pour in milk, return to heat and cook until thickened. Stir in 1/4 cup American cheese and 1/4 cup Cheddar cheese. Cook until cheese melts; set aside. Place one piece of toast each on 4 oven-safe plates; place one slice of turkey on top of each. Cover each with butter mixture; top with remaining cheeses and bacon. Place plates under broiler; broil until bacon is fully cooked. Serves 4.

Vintage swanky swig glasses make the prettiest tea light holders. Their colorful, retro designs really shine through!

Flaky Beef Pie

Jennifer Gubbins
Homewood, IL

Beef, mushrooms and onion in a spicy tomato sauce. You can make individual pies if you use large muffin or Yorkshire pudding tins.

1 lb. ground beef	4-oz. can sliced mushrooms
1 onion, chopped	1 t. salt
1 clove garlic, minced	1 t. chili powder
8-oz. can tomato sauce	2 9-inch pie crusts

Brown beef, onion and garlic in a large skillet; drain. Add tomato sauce, mushrooms, salt and chili powder; heat through. Line a 9" round pie pan with one crust; fill with beef mixture. Cover pie with top crust; crimp and seal edges. Poke several holes in top to allow for steam. Bake at 425 degrees for 20 to 25 minutes. Serves 6 to 8.

Don't save nostalgic pie birds only for fruit pies...they work just as well, and add a little fun, to double-crust beef or chicken pot pies, too!

Gram's Skillet Hash

Shannon Wilson
Newark, OH

*Growing up with 5 brothers, Gram made
this dish quite often.*

1/2 c. onion, chopped
2 T. butter
2 c. ground beef, browned

3 potatoes, peeled and diced
1/2 c. beef broth
1/2 t. salt

Sauté onion in butter in a large skillet; add beef, potatoes, broth and salt. Cook on low heat for 15 to 20 minutes, stirring often. Serves 4.

Delicious Round Steak

Jennifer Gordon
Bainbridge, PA

Serve over steamed rice or buttered noodles.

2 lbs. round steak, cubed
2 10-3/4 oz. cans cream of
   mushroom soup

1/4 t. pepper
1/2 t. salt

Place all ingredients in a slow cooker. Cook on low 6 to 8 hours. Serves 4 to 6.

*Vintage pop bottle crates make terrific garden totes.
Seed packets, small tools and garden gloves
all fit snugly inside.*

Mom's Meatballs

Krista Starnes
Beaufort, SC

This was one of my favorites growing up and I still love the
aroma that fills the house as they simmer on the stove.

1/2 c. instant long-grain rice,
   uncooked
1/2 c. water
1/3 c. onion, chopped
1 t. salt
1/2 t. celery salt
1/8 t. pepper

1/2 t. garlic powder
1 lb. ground beef
2 T. oil
15-oz. can tomato sauce
2 T. brown sugar, packed
2 T. Worcestershire sauce
1 c. water

Combine first 7 ingredients in a large mixing bowl; mix in beef.
Shape into 1-1/2 inch balls; fry in oil until browned. Drain meatballs
on paper towels, then place in a Dutch oven. Combine remaining
ingredients; pour over meatballs. Cover and simmer for one hour.
Serves 4 to 6.

Look for funny-face sock darners the next time
there's a girls' day out antiquing trip. Displayed in a
vintage thread case or basket, they'll make
anyone smile!

Country-Fried Steak

Carol Daugherty
Lexington, OH

*This recipe comes from my family cookbook
that's been enjoyed by 4 generations.*

2 lbs. round steak
1 t. salt
1/4 t. pepper
1 egg
3/4 c. plus 2 T. water, divided
1 c. corn flake cereal, crushed

1 t. chili powder
1/4 c. oil
1 onion, sliced
1 green pepper, sliced
2 8-oz. cans tomato sauce

Flatten steak with a meat mallet; sprinkle with salt and pepper. Beat egg with 2 tablespoons water in a small bowl. In a separate bowl, combine crushed cereal and chili powder. Dip steak into egg mixture, then into cereal mixture. Heat oil in a large skillet; add coated steak and brown on both sides. Add onion, green pepper and tomato sauce; cover and simmer one to 1-1/2 hours or until tender. Makes 5 to 6 servings.

For a fun-filled evening, pull out all the old home movies for a Family Night Movie Marathon...don't forget the popcorn!

Turkey Pot Pie

Mary Wilson
Lansdale, PA

*Served with cranberry relish and a garden salad,
your family will savor every bite!*

1 c. baby carrots
4 stalks celery, chopped
2 potatoes, peeled and cubed
10-1/2 oz. can chicken broth
3 c. milk
1 T. fresh parsley
1 t. fresh rosemary
2 turkey breasts, cubed

1 T. olive oil
1 onion, chopped
6 T. butter
1/3 c. all-purpose flour
salt and pepper to taste
1 c. frozen peas, thawed
  and drained
7-oz. pkg. pie crust mix

Combine carrots, celery, potatoes and broth in a saucepan; bring to a
boil. Cover; cook for 10 minutes. Remove from heat and drain; place
cooked vegetables in a bowl and set aside. Scald milk in saucepan; stir
in parsley and rosemary. Remove from heat and set aside. In a skillet,
brown turkey in olive oil; stir in with vegetables. Sauté onion; add to
vegetables. Melt butter, whisk in flour and cook until golden-brown.
Whisk in scalded milk mixture; cook and stir until thick and bubbly.
Sprinkle in salt and pepper; pour into a greased 13"x9" baking pan.
Lay vegetables and peas on top; toss to coat. Prepare pie crust
according to package directions; roll dough out to fit the top of the
dish. Seal edges; place two cuts in the top to allow for steam. Bake at
375 degrees for 35 to 40 minutes. Serves 6 to 8.

*Seashells gathered from a
vacation at the beach
always bring back
fond memories.
Show them off in a sand
pail decoupaged with
postcards from the same
vacation spot.*

Delicious Chicken & Gravy

Lori Huebsch
Silverton, OR

*Pop it in the oven and, in an hour, you can be sitting down
to a tender chicken dinner.*

3 boneless, skinless chicken
   breasts
2 T. olive oil
10-3/4 oz. can cream of
   mushroom soup

1-1/2 c. sour cream
4 to 5 mushrooms, sliced
2/3 c. beef broth

Brown chicken breasts in olive oil; place in a greased 13"x9" baking
pan. Mix together remaining ingredients; pour over chicken. Bake at
325 degrees for one hour. Serves 2 to 3.

Chicken Sandwich Spread

Jen Licon-Conner
Gooseberry Patch

Use thick slices of Texas toast for a sandwich that's a handful.

2 eggs, hard-boiled and peeled
1 t. butter, melted
1 t. lemon juice
1 c. chicken, cooked and diced

1 t. chicken broth
salt and pepper to taste
4 slices bread

Remove yolks from eggs, reserving whites for another recipe. Mash
yolks and add butter and lemon juice; mix well. Mix in chicken, broth,
salt and pepper. Spread 1/2 cup mixture on 2 bread slices; top with
remaining bread slices. Makes 2 sandwiches.

*Toting a casserole to a get-together? Wrap it up in a
cheery bandanna and tie the knot at the top...an
ideal spot to slip in a serving spoon!*

Slow-Cooker Italian Beef

Linda Hendrix
Moundville, MO

I like to serve this smothered with sautéed onions, green peppers, mushrooms and cheese.

3 to 4-lb. beef chuck roast, trimmed
1-oz. pkg. Italian salad dressing mix
2 t. Italian seasoning

8 oz. pepperoncini peppers
10-1/2 oz. can beef broth
pepper and garlic powder to taste
6 to 8 Kaiser rolls, toasted

Combine first 6 ingredients in a slow cooker. Cook on low 6 to 8 hours. Remove meat, shred and return to slow cooker until ready to serve. Serve on toasted rolls, using juice for dipping. Makes 6 to 8 sandwiches.

A pair of pink flamingos, roosters or swans wouldn't normally be welcome at dinner...but when they're old-fashioned salt & pepper shakers, they add lots of whimsy!

Apricot Chicken

Julie Grose
Granada Hills, CA

The sweet flavor of apricot jam really adds to the chicken.
It's great with rice pilaf or a baked potato on the side.

6 chicken breasts
1 c. apricot jam
1-1/2 oz. pkg. onion soup mix

8-oz. bottle French salad
dressing

Place chicken, skin-side up, in an ungreased 13"x9" baking pan; set aside. Mix remaining ingredients together; pour over chicken. Cover; bake at 375 degrees for 50 minutes. Uncover and bake an additional 20 to 30 minutes, spooning sauce over chicken every 5 minutes. Serves 6.

Potted placecards...pick up some herb seedlings, plant them in tiny terra cotta pots and add popsicle-stick markers with each guest's name. Not only clever, but everyone gets to take one home!

Ham & Scalloped Potatoes

Cathy Webster
Poughkeepsie, NY

A slow-cooker dinner that will stick to your ribs!

3 lbs. redskin potatoes, cubed
    and divided
1-lb. ham steak, cubed and
    divided
2 c. sharp white Cheddar cheese,
    shredded and divided

1 onion, diced and divided
1/4 c. butter, sliced and divided
salt and pepper to taste
2 T. all-purpose flour, divided
1 c. milk

Spray slow cooker with non-stick vegetable spray. Layer half of the potatoes, ham, cheese, onion and butter. Sprinkle with salt, pepper and one tablespoon flour. Repeat all layers; pour milk over top. Cook on high 5 to 6 hours. Serves 4 to 6.

Give an empty corner a cottage feel in no time. Tuck lots of pretty seed packets in old shutters then prop the shutters in a corner...oh-so simple!

North Carolina-Style Barbecue

Patricia Trench
Panama City, FL

Baked in a sweet, brown sugar sauce...just spoon on soft dinner rolls for a hearty dinner sandwich.

4 to 5-lb. pork roast, trimmed
1 onion, chopped
1-1/2 c. water
1 c. vinegar
1/2 c. catsup
1/2 c. Worcestershire sauce

3 T. brown sugar, packed
2 T. dry mustard
1 t. salt
1/4 t. red pepper flakes
1/4 t. pepper

Place roast in a large roasting pan; set aside. Mix remaining ingredients together; pour over roast. Bake at 325 degrees for 5 to 6 hours. Remove roast from sauce; place sauce in refrigerator, removing fat when formed. Remove meat from bone and shred. Return to sauce in pan; bake an additional 15 minutes at 325 degrees or until heated through. Serves 8.

Flea markets often have old bikes for sale. Snap one up, add a bike basket and fill it to the brim with flowering annuals...a surprise in any garden!

Meat Loaf Pie

Wendy Lee Paffenroth
Pine Island, NY

A spin on traditional baked meat loaf...it's round, topped with cheese and cut into wedges before serving.

2 lbs. ground beef
1 onion, chopped
1 green pepper, chopped
1/2 c. catsup
1 t. mustard
1/2 c. quick-cooking oats,
    uncooked

1 c. Italian bread crumbs
1 egg
1/4 c. water
1 t. Worcestershire sauce
4 slices American cheese

Blend together all ingredients, except cheese; place in an ungreased 9" deep-dish pie pan. Smooth over cracks and seams. Bake at 350 degrees for one hour. Cut each slice of cheese, corner to corner, to form 8 triangles; arrange on top of pie. Return to oven for 3 to 4 minutes until cheese melts. Serves 6.

Stacked tin picnic baskets are so handy for tucking favorite cookbooks in!

Pop's Spaghetti Sauce

Marshall Williams
Westerville, OH

Pop was a cook in the Navy during World War II where he learned to cook delicious meals like this spaghetti sauce.

1-1/2 to 2 lbs. ground beef
2 green peppers, chopped
2 onions, chopped
1/2 stalk celery, chopped
2 bay leaves
2 cloves garlic, minced
1-1/2 t. dried oregano
1-1/2 t. dried thyme
1-1/2 t. Italian seasoning
1-1/2 t. dried basil

1-1/2 t. pepper
2 t. salt
1 T. sugar
6-oz. can tomato paste
2 15-oz. cans chunky
   tomato sauce
1/2 c. water
1 T. olive oil
8-oz. can sliced mushrooms

Brown beef in a large saucepan, separating beef into small pieces; drain. Combine peppers, onions, celery and beef in a large stockpot. In a separate bowl, mix together remaining ingredients; add to beef mixture. Simmer over low heat for 3 to 4 hours, stirring occasionally; remove bay leaves. Serve over cooked pasta. Makes 6 to 8 servings.

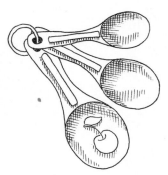

Ice cream parlor chairs add a touch of charm wherever they sit...at a desk, in a little girl's room or outside on the porch. After a fresh coat of paint, add a stencil on the seat for added charm.

Stuffed Cabbage Rolls

*Paula Spadaccini
Shelburne, VT*

A sprinkling of gingersnaps gives these a hint of ginger.

1 head cabbage
2 onions, sliced
4 carrots, peeled and sliced
1 lb. ground beef
1/4 c. instant rice, uncooked
1/4 c. catsup
2 15-oz. cans tomato sauce

10-3/4 oz. can cream of
   tomato soup
1/2 c. brown sugar, packed
2 T. lemon juice
salt and pepper to taste
10 to 12 gingersnaps, crushed

Bring a large pot of water to boil; lower cabbage into pot. Cook for
10 minutes; remove. Peel off 12 outer leaves; set aside. Place onions
and carrots in the bottom of a Dutch oven; set aside. Mix beef, rice
and catsup together; form into 12 balls. Wrap each ball in a cabbage
leaf; place on top of vegetables in Dutch oven. Mix together tomato
sauce, tomato soup, brown sugar, lemon juice, salt and pepper; pour
over rolls. Add enough water to cover rolls; cover. Bake at 350 degrees
for 2 hours; remove cover and sprinkle with gingersnaps. Serves 12.

*In a pinch for time? Here's a
shortcut for making cabbage
rolls. Instead of filling each
leaf, shred and cook cabbage
and lay in a
2-quart baking dish. Add
the beef and rice mixture,
and then top with brown
sugar sauce.*

Cheesy Tuna Melt

Cindy Watson
Gooseberry Patch

Terrific with French fries or crispy onion rings.

2 6-oz. cans tuna, drained
4 eggs, hard-boiled, peeled
   and chopped
1/2 c. olives, sliced
3 T. onion, minced

2/3 c. mayonnaise
24 slices bread, crusts trimmed
1/2 c. butter, softened
5-oz. jar sharp Cheddar cheese
   spread, softened

Combine first 5 ingredients. Spread 12 bread slices with tuna mixture; top with remaining slices. Blend together butter and cheese; lightly spread over tops of sandwiches. Arrange on an ungreased baking sheet; cover and refrigerate overnight. Remove cover and bake at 400 degrees for 10 minutes until golden. Makes 12 sandwiches.

*Serve up hearty sandwiches outside in warm weather.
An old wooden fruit crate serves as a sturdy tray
with plenty of room for dinner plus a
frosty bottle of soda!*

Quick Salmon Patties

Bonnie Yeska
Hinsdale, MT

*Quick Salmon Patties make it easy to have dinner ready in a flash.
They're great paired with a steamed fresh vegetable.*

2 14-3/4 oz. cans salmon,
   bones removed
1 onion, chopped
30 saltine crackers, crushed

3 eggs
1/8 t. pepper
1/8 t. salt

Spray skillet with non-stick vegetable spray. Combine all ingredients in a mixing bowl. Form into 6 patties. Place in skillet; cook until lightly golden on each side. Serves 6.

Chicken Cacciatore

Jennifer Minekheim
Garden Grove, CA

If you shy away from garlic, you can always leave it out.

1 lb. chicken breasts, cubed
2 T. oil
28-oz. jar spaghetti sauce
14-1/2 oz. jar canned tomatoes
1 green pepper, chopped

1 onion, chopped
2 cloves garlic, minced
1 t. Italian seasoning
salt and pepper to taste

Brown chicken in oil in a large skillet. Add spaghetti sauce and stir in remaining ingredients. Simmer until vegetables are tender. Serves 2 to 4.

Color copies of vintage fabrics make terrific one-of-a-kind stationery, scrapbook pages, envelopes or gift tags!

Upside-Down Pizza

Jan Fishback
Carmi, IL

The meat and vegetables can be adapted to anyone's tastes...try sausage or pepperoni with green peppers.

2 lbs. ground beef
1 onion, chopped
4-oz. can sliced mushrooms
1-1/4 oz. pkg. dry spaghetti
   sauce mix

2 8-oz. cans tomato sauce
1 c. sour cream
2 c. shredded mozzarella cheese
8-oz. tube refrigerated
   crescent rolls

Brown beef, onion and mushrooms in a large skillet; drain well. Stir in sauce mix and tomato sauce; pour into an ungreased 13"x9" baking pan. Spread sour cream over top. Sprinkle with cheese. Roll out crescent dough; pinch seams closed. Stretch dough to fit over top of pan, touching all edges. Bake at 350 degrees for 30 minutes. Let stand several minutes before serving. Serves 6.

An old wooden ladder provides great kitchen storage...lean it against the wall to hold dish towels, tablecloths or aprons.

Mom's Hamburger Stroganoff

*Laura Strausberger
Roswell, GA*

You don't need a lot of time to make this handed-down recipe.

1/2 c. onion, minced
1 clove garlic, minced
1/4 c. butter
1 lb. ground beef
2 T. all-purpose flour
2 t. salt
1/4 t. pepper

1 lb. sliced mushrooms
10-3/4 oz. can cream of chicken
   soup
1 c. sour cream
2 T. fresh parsley, minced
12-oz. pkg. wide egg noodles,
   cooked

Sauté onion and garlic in butter over medium heat. Add beef and cook until browned. Add flour, salt, pepper and mushrooms; cook for 5 minutes. Stir in soup; simmer 10 additional minutes. Stir in sour cream and heat through. Sprinkle with parsley and serve over prepared noodles. Makes 4 to 6 servings.

Discount stores have lots of vintage-style cotton tea towels that make cheery window valances!

Old-Fashioned Fried Chicken

Char Thomas
New Hope, MN

Remember all the good things that go with this...cole slaw,
baked beans, mashed potatoes and biscuits.

1 gal. cold water
1 c. kosher salt
1 c. sugar
4 to 5 lbs. chicken

1 c. all-purpose flour
3/4 c. buttermilk
1/2 t. cayenne pepper
oil for deep frying

Combine water, salt and sugar in a large bowl; add chicken. Cover and
refrigerate overnight; drain and pat dry. Combine flour, buttermilk and
pepper in a mixing bowl. Coat each piece of chicken; deep fry in oil at
355 degrees for 8 minutes or until juices run clear. Makes 4 to
6 servings.

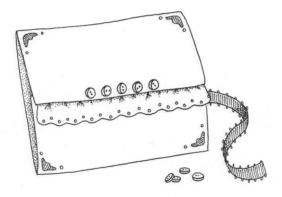

Teeny, tiny buttons found at antique shops may
look too small to really use, but what would be
sweeter glued to the front a baby announcement?
Rubber stamp the inside (using blue or pink ink) to
share the happy news with family & friends!

Dried Beef Hot Dish

Beth Goblirsch
Minneapolis, MN

This was one of my mom's stand-by recipes. I remember her bringing it to picnics and potlucks while I was growing up.

1 c. milk
10-3/4 oz. can cream of
   mushroom soup
1 c. shredded Cheddar cheese
1 c. elbow macaroni, uncooked

3 T. onion, chopped
1/4 c. chopped dried beef
2 eggs, hard-boiled, peeled
   and sliced

Combine all ingredients in an ungreased 1-1/2 quart baking dish. Refrigerate 3 to 4 hours or overnight. Bake at 350 degrees for one hour. Serves 4.

What an entrance! Create a family picture swag by cutting a length of jute to hang across a doorway. Use clothespins to hold photos...looks great over a mirror too.

Swedish Meatballs

Rita Anderson
Mechanicsburg, OH

Pineapple juice in the sauce gives this classic a sweet and tangy taste. Just serve over steamed rice for a complete meal.

1 lb. ground beef	1 t. salt
1/4 lb. ground sausage	1 T. onion, chopped
1 egg	1/2 c. crackers, crushed
1 T. cornstarch	oil for frying

Mix together first 7 ingredients. Form into 1-1/2 inch balls. Brown in oil, turning often. Serve with sauce. Makes 4 to 6 servings.

Sauce:

1 T. oil	3 T. cornstarch
1 c. pineapple juice	1 T. soy sauce
6 T. water	3 T. vinegar
1/2 c. sugar	

Combine all ingredients in a saucepan; cook over low heat until thick.

Make a real family tree by planting a tree for someone special every year. In Autumn there are some terrific sales at garden centers...the perfect time to shop and plant!

COUNTRY
Casseroles to Share

Grandma's Chicken Casserole

Ashley Trueblood
Glendale, AZ

This is my favorite casserole and one that my grandmother used to make. The different combination of ingredients tastes delicious.

2 3 to 4-lb. chickens, cooked
   and boned
1 c. celery, chopped
1/3 c. French salad dressing
1 T. mustard
1 c. sour cream

1/2 c. slivered almonds
1 c. shredded Cheddar cheese
10-3/4 oz. can cream of
   celery soup
1 onion, quartered

Tear chicken into bite-size pieces; place in a large mixing bowl. Add celery, dressing, mustard, sour cream, almonds and cheese; set aside. Mix together soup and onion in a food processor; add to chicken mixture. Pour into an ungreased 3-quart baking dish; bake at 350 degrees for 30 minutes. Serves 6 to 8.

Chicken with twice the flavor! Let it cool in its broth before cutting or shredding for casseroles.

Johnny Marzetti

Linda Karner
Pisgah Forest, NC

The name for this combination of tasty ingredients originated in the 1920's, at a restaurant in Ohio called Marzetti's. Johnny was the brother of founder Teresa Marzetti. The restaurant is long gone, but its name remains, on her brother's favorite dish.

2 T. oil
1 onion, chopped
1 green pepper, chopped
1 lb. ground beef
28-oz. jar spaghetti sauce
1-1/2 c. prepared elbow
   macaroni
2 c. shredded Cheddar cheese

Heat oil in a skillet. Add onion and green pepper; sauté until softened. Add ground beef; cook until beef is browned. Stir in spaghetti sauce and macaroni; pour in an ungreased 13"x9" baking pan. Sprinkle with cheese. Bake at 350 degrees for one hour. Serves 4 to 6.

Keep pasta from boiling over by coating the lid with a little vegetable oil or laying a metal spatula across the top of the stockpot.

Traditional Lasagna

Pat Husek
St. Joseph, MI

It's simple to make lasagna ahead of time and freeze for a later date. Just pop it in the oven and bake, covered, for 30 minutes. Uncover, and continue baking for about 45 minutes or until the center is steaming.

1-1/2 lbs. ground beef
1/2 lb. ground sausage
2 14-1/2 oz. cans diced
    tomatoes
8-oz. can tomato sauce
1 t. dried oregano
1/4 t. dried thyme

salt and pepper to taste
10 lasagna noodles, cooked
    and divided
8-oz. pkg. shredded mozzarella
    cheese, divided
grated Parmesan cheese to taste

Brown beef and sausage together; add tomatoes, tomato sauce, oregano, thyme, salt and pepper. In an ungreased 13"x9" baking pan, layer half sauce mixture, 5 noodles, and half mozzarella cheese; repeat layering. Top with Parmesan cheese. Bake at 350 degrees for one hour. Serves 6 to 8.

A pretty serving tray can be made from a large picture frame in no time. Decoupage images from vintage magazines, dress patterns and cards on the back of the frame and let dry. Replace the glass in the frame and it's done!

Layered Ravioli Bake

Carolann McCartney
Binghamton, NY

Quick and so simple to make...great for a crowd!

26-oz. jar spaghetti sauce,
    divided
26-oz. pkg. frozen
    ravioli, divided

1 lb. ground beef, browned
    and divided
8-oz. pkg. shredded
    mozzarella cheese, divided

Layer one cup spaghetti sauce, half the ravioli, half the ground beef and half the cheese in an ungreased 11"x7" baking pan. Repeat layering; bake at 425 degrees for 30 to 35 minutes. Serves 4 to 6.

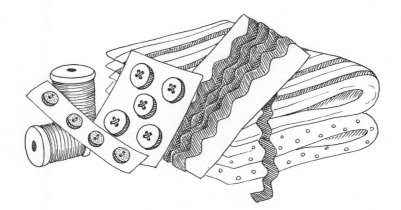

Games from the 1940's and 1950's were fun and really brought families together. Still available at flea markets and auctions, treat yourself and plan a Family Game Night!

Chicken & Vegetable Bake

Bobbi-Jo Thornton
Caribou, ME

*Here's a dish you can rely on when you're having company,
but don't have a lot of time to cook.*

4 boneless, skinless chicken
   breasts
1 zucchini, peeled and chopped
1 yellow squash, chopped
1 c. baby carrots, chopped
1 onion, chopped

1 red pepper, chopped
1/4 c. olive oil
1 t. dried parsley
1 t. dried marjoram
1 t. dried thyme
16-oz. can chopped tomatoes

Place chicken, zucchini, squash, carrots, onion and pepper in an
ungreased 13"x9" baking pan; set aside. Mix together olive oil and
herbs; pour over chicken. Cover and bake at 350 degrees for
45 minutes. Uncover and pour tomatoes on top; bake an additional
10 minutes. Serves 4.

*What a time saver! Most casseroles can be prepared
the night before; just cover and refrigerate.
When it's ready to be baked, simply add
15 to 20 minutes to the original baking time.*

Grandma McCall's Noodle Casserole

Aryn Lentz
Camp Hill, PA

Canned soup makes this a snap to prepare.

10-oz. pkg. wide egg noodles
10-3/4 oz. can golden
   mushroom soup
1 lb. ground beef

salt and pepper to taste
10-3/4 oz. can French onion
   soup
water

Prepare noodles according to package directions; drain. Mix in mushroom soup and set aside. Brown beef in a skillet; salt and pepper to taste. Drain and pour into a lightly greased 13"x9" baking pan. Layer noodles and French onion soup over top. Fill 1/2 soup can with water; pour over top. Bake at 375 degrees for 40 minutes. Serves 6 to 8.

Tired of misplacing the recipe while preparing a dish? Slip the recipe card in fork tines and then stand the fork in a glass...so easy!

Creamy Tuna Casserole

Lisa Bracken
Elizabethtown, KY

Kids in grade school used to call this Tuna-Pea Wiggle!

6-1/2 oz. can tuna, drained
10-3/4 oz. can cream of
   mushroom soup
2 T. mayonnaise
1 T. mayonnaise-type
   salad dressing
milk

2 T. onion, chopped
15-1/4 oz. can peas, drained
8-oz. pkg. wide egg noodles,
   cooked
1/2 c. shredded Cheddar cheese
1-1/2 c. potato chips, crushed

Mix together tuna, soup, mayonnaise, salad dressing, one soup can of milk and onion in a greased 2-quart casserole dish. Stir in peas and noodles; sprinkle with cheese and potato chips. Bake in a 375-degree oven for 25 to 30 minutes or until bubbly. Serves 4 to 6.

Keep recipe cards nice and dry while cooking...just seal between 2 sheets of laminating paper.

Hearty Stuffed Pepper Casserole

Vickie

Love stuffed peppers? Try this casserole version for a new family favorite!

2-1/2 c. herb-flavored stuffing
    mix, divided
1 T. butter, melted
1 lb. ground beef
1/2 c. onion, chopped

14-1/2 oz. can whole tomatoes,
    chopped
8-oz. can corn, drained
salt and pepper to taste
2 green peppers, quartered

Mix together 1/4 cup stuffing mix and butter; set aside. Brown beef and onion in a medium skillet over medium-high heat; drain well. Stir in tomatoes, corn, salt and pepper; mix in remaining stuffing. Arrange peppers in an ungreased 2-quart baking dish; spoon beef mixture over top. Cover and bake at 400 degrees for 25 minutes. Sprinkle with reserved stuffing mixture. Bake, uncovered, for 5 additional minutes or until peppers are tender. Serves 4 to 6.

Sharing a casserole? Be sure to tie on a tag with the recipe. Clever tags can be made from almost anything...mailing or gift tags, decorative notecards, ribbons and colorful labels!

Mushroom & Barley Casserole

Betty Pippin
Albany, GA

Try substituting peas and cashews for the mushrooms and onions...it's just as good.

1/2 c. pearled barley, uncooked
1/2 c. onion, chopped
3 T. butter, melted
8-oz. can chicken broth
4-1/2 oz. can mushrooms
1/2 c. sliced almonds

Brown barley and onion in butter; stirring constantly. Add remaining ingredients; spoon into an ungreased 1-1/2 quart baking dish. Bake at 350 degrees for one hour and 15 minutes. Serves 4.

Cauliflower-Ham Au Gratin

Kristie Rigo
Friedens, PA

Hot, bubbly and golden!

2 10-oz. pkgs. frozen
   cauliflower, thawed
1-1/4 c. smoked ham, chopped
10-3/4 oz. can Cheddar cheese
   soup
1/4 c. milk
2/3 c. biscuit baking mix
2 T. butter, softened
2 T. shredded Cheddar cheese

Arrange cauliflower in an ungreased 13"x9" baking pan; sprinkle with ham. Mix soup and milk until smooth; pour over ham. Combine remaining ingredients; sprinkle over soup mixture. Bake at 400 degrees for 25 to 30 minutes. Serves 4 to 6.

There is no instinct like that of the heart.
-Lord Byron

Herbed Squash Casserole

Carol Hickman
Kingsport, TN

*There're lots of different types of squash and each is so easy to grow;
why not add a plant or two to your vegetable garden this year?*

4 c. yellow squash, sliced
1 onion, chopped
2 T. butter
3 c. herb-flavored bread crumbs
1/2 c. margarine, melted
2 c. sour cream

8-oz. can golden
   mushroom soup
1 t. salt
1/2 t. pepper
2 carrots, grated

Sauté squash and onion in butter until tender; drain. Mix together bread crumbs and margarine; place half of mixture in the bottom of a 13"x9" baking pan. Spread squash and onions over top; set aside. In a bowl, mix together sour cream, soup, salt, pepper and carrots; pour over squash. Top with remaining bread crumb mixture; bake at 350 degrees for 30 minutes. Serves 6.

Sharing a casserole with a new mom? Bake it in a pretty speckled enamelware pan and make the pan part of her gift. It's sure to come in handy for lots of family dinners!

Creamy Sausage-Rice Bake

Kathleen Eaton
Middletown, DE

Use hot sausage if you want a casserole with a little kick.

2 lbs. ground sausage, browned
2 onions, chopped
1/2 c. green peppers, chopped
1 c. celery, chopped
1 c. instant rice, uncooked
10-3/4 oz. can chicken
    gumbo soup

10-3/4 oz. can cream of
    chicken soup
2 c. water
8-oz. pkg. shredded
    Cheddar cheese

Combine sausage, onions, green pepper and celery in a large skillet; sauté 2 to 3 minutes. Drain if necessary. Add all remaining ingredients, stirring to blend. Spoon into an ungreased 2-1/2 quart baking dish. Bake, covered, for 1-1/2 hours. Serves 4 to 6.

Here's a handy tip to keep casseroles from bubbling over...just slide a toothpick between the casserole dish and the lid. The steam escapes and the oven stays clean!

Chicken Crunch Supreme

Lori Maynor
El Dorado, AR

Taking this to a potluck? Be prepared to share the recipe!

2 c. chicken, cooked and cubed
1/4 c. celery, diced
1 t. dried, minced onion
10-3/4 oz. can cream of
    mushroom soup
1-1/2 c. prepared thin egg
    noodles

1 c. shredded Cheddar cheese
1/3 c. mayonnaise
8-oz. can water chestnuts
salt and pepper to taste
2 c. corn flake cereal, crushed
1/3 c. sliced almonds
1/4 c. butter, melted

Mix together chicken, celery, onion, soup, noodles, cheese, mayonnaise, water chestnuts, salt and pepper; place in an ungreased 9"x9" baking pan. Top with cereal and almonds; drizzle with butter. Bake, covered, at 375 degrees for 50 minutes; uncover and bake for an additional 10 minutes. Serves 4 to 6.

When it's time for the family reunion, send out "Save this Date" cards several weeks in advance. This way, everyone will remember to mark their calendars and not miss all the fun!

Hearty Beef Stew Casserole

Judy Davis
Muskogee, OK

*When you're looking for a quick comfort food,
look no further...this is it.*

3 c. mashed potatoes
1 lb. ground beef
salt and pepper to taste
2 t. garlic powder
2 t. onion powder

15-oz. can beef stew
10-3/4 oz. can cream of
   mushroom soup
1/2 c. water

Spread mashed potatoes in a buttered 2-quart microwave-safe dish; set aside. Brown ground beef in a skillet; salt and pepper to taste. Season with garlic and onion powder; drain well. Over medium heat, add stew, soup and water to beef; mix thoroughly and heat through. Pour mixture over potatoes. Microwave on high for 5 minutes. Serves 4 to 6.

If time's short, pick up packaged mashed potatoes at the grocery store for Hearty Beef Stew Casserole. They can even be bought "with lumps" so they taste more homemade!

Cheesy Zucchini Casserole

Deborah Patterson
Carmichael, CA

Treat yourself to extra helpings!

2 lbs. zucchini, sliced
1 c. prepared rice
2 eggs, beaten
1 c. mushroom soup

salt and pepper to taste
1-1/2 c. shredded Cheddar
    cheese

Place zucchini in a saucepan; cover with water. Boil until tender; drain and mash. Mix together rice, eggs and soup; add zucchini, salt and pepper. Layer rice mixture and cheese in a greased 1-1/2 quart baking dish; Bake at 350 degrees for 30 to 40 minutes. Serves 6.

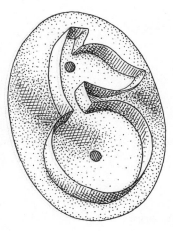

Pick up an old-fashioned medicine chest at the next tag sale...it makes a great place to store spices. Adhesive-backed cork attached to the mirror makes keeping track of shopping lists easy!

Corned Beef Casserole

Jessica Heaton
Cedar Grove, WI

Tasty with corn muffins and sweet butter.

12-oz. can corned beef
10-3/4 oz. can cream of
  chicken soup
10-oz. pkg. elbow macaroni,
  cooked

5-oz. can evaporated milk
8-oz. pkg. Cheddar cheese,
  cubed
1/4 t. onion powder

Mix all ingredients together; pour into a greased 13"x9" baking pan. Bake at 350 degrees for 45 minutes. Serves 6 to 8.

Cornbread Stuffing

Tracy Tregle
LaPlace, LA

Moist and delicious.

1 onion, chopped
1 T. garlic, minced
1 green pepper, chopped
1 T. oil
1 lb. ground beef

salt and pepper to taste
8-1/2 oz. pkg. cornbread mix,
  prepared and crumbled
10-1/2 oz. can chicken broth

Sauté onion, garlic and pepper in oil for 5 minutes. Add beef, season with salt and pepper and cook until browned; drain. Stir in cornbread, then spoon mixture into a lightly greased 13"x9" baking pan. Pour broth over top; bake at 350 degrees for 30 minutes. Makes about 8 servings.

Creamy Herb Pasta Bake

Deanna Arnold
Columbia City, IN

Add a crisp salad and some garlic bread for a complete meal.

1 T. oil
2 to 3 boneless, skinless chicken
   breasts, diced
8-oz. pkg. fettuccine, cooked
26-oz. jar spaghetti sauce
14-1/2 oz. can diced tomatoes

10-3/4 oz. can cream of chicken
   and herb soup
1 c. shredded mozzarella cheese
1/3 c. grated Parmesan cheese
1/3 c. Italian bread crumbs

Heat oil in a skillet; add diced chicken. Cook and toss until chicken is cooked through, about 10 minutes. Drain and set aside. Rinse cooked pasta with cold water. In a large mixing bowl, blend together spaghetti sauce, tomatoes and soup. Stir in chicken and pasta; spread into a lightly greased 2-quart baking dish. Sprinkle mozzarella cheese evenly over top. In a small bowl, toss together Parmesan cheese and bread crumbs. Sprinkle on top of casserole. Bake at 375 degrees for 35 to 45 minutes or until golden and bubbly. Serves 4 to 6.

Keep tiny pots of fresh herbs on the kitchen windowsill...they'll be right at your fingertips for any recipe!

Shepherd's Pie

Jo Ann

This dish was typically eaten on Monday...a way to use leftover beef and potatoes from Sunday dinner.

1 lb. ground beef
1 T. oil
1 clove garlic, chopped
2 shallots, sliced
1 onion, chopped
1 t. salt
1 t. pepper
2 T. all-purpose flour

1 c. beef broth
1 T. tomato paste
1 c. frozen peas, thawed
2 T. fresh parsley, chopped
4 c. mashed potatoes
1 c. shredded Cheddar cheese
1/4 c. grated Parmesan cheese

Brown beef in oil with garlic, shallots and onion. Add salt, pepper and flour and continue cooking 3 to 4 minutes. Add beef broth and tomato paste, stirring until mixture becomes creamy. Add peas and parsley, cooking through. Pour mixture into an ungreased 13"x9" baking pan; spread mashed potatoes over top and sprinkle cheeses over potatoes. Bake at 400 degrees for 20 minutes until golden. Serves 6 to 8.

Table tents are so handy! Fold a piece of paper in half and jot down or rubber stamp the recipe name on one side. Set the table tent next to a casserole dish so everyone will know just what's inside!

Velvety Hashbrown Casserole

Gloria Kaufmann
Orrville, OH

Not just a "regular" hashbrown casserole...this has a buttery, Parmesan cheese sauce.

3 12-oz. pkgs. frozen shredded
     hashbrowns
1 qt. half-and-half
1/2 c. margarine

1 t. salt
1/8 t. pepper
1/3 c. grated Parmesan cheese

Thaw hashbrowns; combine with all ingredients, except Parmesan cheese. Pour into a lightly greased 13"x9" baking pan. Sprinkle Parmesan cheese over top. Bake at 350 degrees for one hour. Makes 8 to 10 servings.

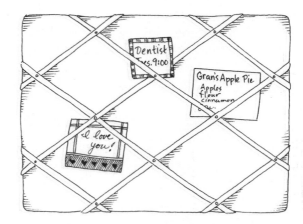

Make a ribbon board to keep recipes, invitations and postcards organized. Use spray adhesive to cover a piece of foam core with fabric and then weave a pattern with ribbon. Secure the ribbon pattern with whimsical tacks and it's ready in no time!

3-Cheese Ziti

Terry Esposito
Freehold, NJ

The secret's in the variety of cheeses!

3 c. ricotta cheese
1 T. dried parsley
1-1/2 t. salt
1 egg
10-oz. pkg. frozen chopped
   spinach, cooked
1/3 c. grated Parmesan cheese

26-oz. jar spaghetti sauce,
   divided
16-oz. pkg. ziti, cooked
   and divided
16-oz. pkg. shredded mozzarella
   cheese, divided

Blend together ricotta cheese, parsley, salt, egg and spinach; puree until smooth. Add Parmesan cheese, blending to combine. Spread enough spaghetti sauce in an ungreased 13"x9" baking pan to cover the bottom. Arrange half pasta over sauce; spread with half ricotta cheese mixture. Cover with half remaining sauce; sprinkle half mozzarella cheese on top. Repeat layers, ending with mozzarella cheese. Bake at 350 degrees for 45 minutes. Serves 6 to 8.

Spend time cuddled up on the porch swing...a simple country pleasure.

Hot Chicken Salad

Karen Hoag
Jackson, NE

*Add a crunchy topping of crushed potato chips, buttery crackers
or bread crumbs if you'd like.*

4 c. chicken, cooked and diced
1/2 c. green onions, chopped
1 c. celery, chopped
2/3 c. slivered almonds
1/4 c. olives, sliced

10-3/4 oz. can cream of
    chicken soup
1 c. mayonnaise
1 t. lemon juice
2 c. shredded Cheddar cheese

Combine all ingredients, except cheese; mix well. Spread into an
ungreased 13"x9" baking pan; sprinkle cheese over top. Bake at
325 degrees for 25 minutes until cheese is melted and bubbly. Serves
10 to 12.

Ham & Cheddar Quiche

Barbara Parish
Martinez, GA

You can't go wrong with this...it's a classic.

4 eggs, beaten
1 c. milk
1/8 t. pepper
1/4 t. salt

1 c. cooked ham, diced
1/2 lb. shredded sharp
    Cheddar cheese
9-inch deep-dish pie crust

Combine eggs, milk, pepper, salt, ham and cheese; mix well. Pour into
pie crust; bake at 350 degrees for 45 to 50 minutes. Serves 6 to 8.

*A friendship box is a sweet way to say "thanks."
Paint a paper maché box and cover the lid with
vintage buttons, fabric snippets, charms and
a favorite photograph of the two of you.*

Cheese & Onion Casserole

JoAnne Cripps
Belding, MI

Definitely for onion lovers!

1-1/2 c. shredded
   Cheddar cheese
1/2 t. salt
3/4 c. all-purpose flour
1/2 c. butter, melted
2 onions, cut into rings
1 T. butter

1/2 c. Swiss cheese, grated
2 eggs
1 c. half-and-half
1/8 t. salt
1/2 t. dry mustard
2 T. grated Parmesan cheese
paprika to taste

Mix together first 4 ingredients; press into a lightly greased
13"x9" baking pan. Sauté onion rings in butter; arrange over crust.
Combine Swiss cheese, eggs, half-and-half, salt and mustard; pour
over onions. Sprinkle Parmesan cheese and paprika over top. Bake at
400 degrees for 15 minutes. Reduce temperature to 325 degrees and
continue baking for 40 to 45 minutes. Makes 8 to 10 servings.

*Make a charming
keepsake from
Grandma's worn
quilts...stitch the
prettiest pieces into
a pincushion or
postcard-size pillow.*

Golden Macaroni & Cheese

Gale Harris
Fort Worth, TX

A topping of crispy, French-fried onions gives this traditional stand-by extra crunch!

10-3/4 oz. can cream of
  mushroom soup
1/2 c. milk
1/2 t. mustard
1/8 t. pepper

3 c. prepared elbow macaroni
2 c. shredded Cheddar
  cheese, divided
1 c. French-fried onions

Blend soup, milk, mustard and pepper in a lightly greased 1-1/2 quart baking dish. Stir in macaroni and 1-1/2 cups cheese. Bake at 350 degrees for 20 minutes. Top with remaining cheese and onions; bake 10 additional minutes. Serves 4.

Help a potluck hostess keep track of all the casserole dishes...jot down your name on a piece of tape or mailing label with a waterproof marker, and then attach it to the bottom of the baking dish.

Poppy Seed Chicken

Hadley Woodard
Henderson, KY

A no-fuss recipe, but it's every bit as delicious as it is convenient.

10-3/4 oz. can cream of
    chicken soup
10-3/4 oz. can cream of
    celery soup
1 c. sour cream
4 to 5 doz. round buttery
    crackers, crushed

1/2 c. butter, melted
1 T. poppy seed
5 boneless, skinless chicken
    breasts, cooked and
    shredded

Mix together soups and sour cream; set aside. In a separate bowl, combine crackers, butter and poppy seed. Layer chicken, soup mixture and crackers in an ungreased 13"x9" baking pan; bake at 350 degrees for 30 minutes. Serves 6 to 8.

There are so many great-tasting cream soups...mushroom, celery, onion and chicken. Shake up an old favorite recipe by trying a different one each time!

Mexican Cornbread Bake

Terri Taylor
Jonesville, LA

Spicy beef tucked between layers of golden cornbread...yum!

1 lb. ground beef
4-1/2 oz. can chopped green
   chilies
1 onion, chopped
2 t. Mexican seasoning

1 T. chili powder
8-oz. can Mexican-style
   tomato sauce
8-1/2 oz. pkg. cornbread mix

Brown beef and drain. Add chilies, onion, seasoning and chili powder;
cook until onions are tender. Add tomato sauce and simmer. Prepare
cornbread batter according to package directions; pour half the batter
into a lightly greased 2-quart baking dish. Spoon beef mixture over
batter; top with remaining cornbread batter. Bake at 350 degrees for
25 to 30 minutes or until the cornbread is golden. Serves 4 to 6.

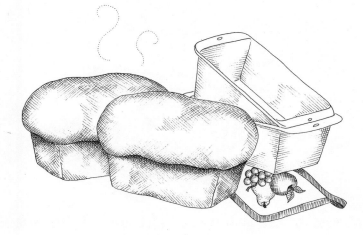

placecards that couldn't be easier...tuck a
rubber-stamped notecard into the sections of
a plump pine cone!

Great-Gran's Corn Casserole

Marge Johnston
Milford, OH

*This was a blue ribbon winner at the local fair in
Gran's day...it always goes fast!*

2 15-1/4 oz. cans corn
8-oz. can water chestnuts, diced
1 onion, chopped
10-3/4 oz. can cream of
    celery soup
1 c. sour cream

1 c. shredded mild
    Cheddar cheese
1 sleeve round buttery crackers,
    crumbled
1/2 c. butter, melted

Combine first 5 ingredients; pour into an ungreased 13"x9" baking
pan. Sprinkle with cheese; spread crushed crackers over top. Drizzle
melted butter evenly over crackers. Bake at 350 degrees for
45 minutes until bubbly and golden. Makes 8 to 10 servings.

*Sometimes a recipe sounds delicious, but serves way
too many people. An easy solution...divide the
casserole into 2 smaller dishes and then bake. Share
the extra with a neighbor or pop it into the freezer
for a quick meal later!*

Simple Cheesy Noodle Bake

Phyllis Peters
Three Rivers, MI

So easy to toss together...what a time saver!

1 lb. ground sirloin, browned
10-oz. pkg. wide egg noodles,
  cooked
10-3/4 oz. can cream of
  celery soup

10-3/4 oz. can cream of
  mushroom soup
1 c. sharp Cheddar
  cheese, divided
5 T. evaporated milk

Mix together sirloin, noodles, soups, 1/2 cup cheese and milk. Pour into a lightly greased 13"x9" baking pan. Sprinkle remaining cheese on top. Bake at 350 degrees for one hour. Serves 8 to 10.

Saucy Sour Cream Casserole

Paula Parent
Agawam, MA

This is one of my family's favorites. The taste is out of this world...not to mention that it's simple to make!

1 lb. ground beef
1 onion, chopped
2 T. butter
salt and pepper to taste
1 t. sugar
2 8-oz. cans tomato sauce

8-oz. pkg. wide egg noodles,
  cooked
3-oz. pkg. cream cheese
1 c. sour cream
1/2 c. shredded Cheddar cheese

Brown beef and onion in butter; add salt, pepper, sugar and tomato sauce. Cover and cook 20 minutes. In a separate bowl, mix together cream cheese and sour cream. In a lightly greased 2-quart baking dish, layer 1/3 noodles, 1/3 cream mixture, 1/3 beef mixture; repeat twice. Top with Cheddar cheese. Cover and bake at 350 degrees for 20 minutes. Serves 6.

Crunchy Onion Casserole

Dianne Button
Newfane, NY

*Don't tell anyone what the secret ingredient is...they'll
be pleasantly surprised!*

2 10-3/4 oz. cans cream of
    mushroom soup
milk
1 t. seasoned salt
1 t. garlic pepper

1 t. paprika
2 onions, diced
2 c. mild Cheddar cheese, grated
14-oz. bag potato chips, crushed

Heat soup in a large saucepan over low heat; fill both soup cans with
milk and add to saucepan. Mix in seasoned salt, garlic pepper and
paprika, stirring until smooth. Pour mixture into a large mixing bowl;
add remaining ingredients. Pour into a 13"x9" baking pan coated with
non-stick vegetable spray. Bake at 300 degrees for one hour until
lightly golden. Makes 6 to 8 servings.

*Keep from crying...place onions in the freezer for
5 minutes and then slice or chop them!*

Chicken Tetrazzini

Debra Donnelly
Pampa, TX

Try substituting ham or turkey for the chicken for a tasty change.

14-1/2 oz. can chicken broth
8-oz. pkg spaghetti, uncooked
1/2 c. onion, diced
1 green pepper, chopped
4-1/2 oz. can sliced mushrooms
2-1/2 c. chicken, cooked
    and diced

2 c. milk
1/2 c. all-purpose flour
2/3 c. margarine, melted
2 c. shredded Cheddar cheese
2/3 c. round buttery crackers,
    crushed

Bring chicken broth to a boil in a stockpot; add spaghetti and cook until tender. Drain and set aside. Combine onion, green pepper and mushrooms in a skillet; cook in mushroom juice until soft. Add vegetables and chicken to cooked spaghetti in a large bowl; mix well and pour in a lightly greased 13"x9" baking pan. In a separate bowl, combine milk, flour, margarine and cheese; pour over spaghetti mixture. Sprinkle crushed crackers over top. Bake at 350 degrees for 50 minutes. Serves 6 to 8.

Shake up a traditional dish for a change of pace. Use fettuccine or angel hair pasta in Chicken Tetrazzini...try rotini or wagon wheel pasta in macaroni & cheese.

Chicken & Rice Bake

Donna Hamilton
Bangs, TX

A tried & true recipe everyone will love.

2 c. instant brown rice, uncooked
1-1/2 oz. pkg. onion soup mix, divided
15-oz. can cream of mushroom soup
15-oz. can cream of chicken soup
1-3/4 c. water
4 boneless, skinless chicken breasts

Combine rice, half onion soup mix, soups and water in a 13"x9" baking pan coated with non-stick cooking spray. Lay chicken breasts on top. Sprinkle remaining onion soup mix over chicken and rice. Bake at 350 degrees for 30 to 45 minutes. Serves 4.

Bring back the good old days...enjoy a nostalgic radio show with the kids! Some radio stations still carry reissues of old classics, but if that's hard to find, pick up cassette tapes at the library. Radio Mystery Theatre, The Adventures of Red Ryder or The Lone Ranger are ones the whole family will love listening to.

Ham & Potatoes Au Gratin

Hope Davenport
Portland, TX

Tender ham and potatoes in a creamy sauce. This recipe takes almost no preparation time...ideal for a busy family.

2-lb. bag frozen shredded
    hashbrowns, thawed
2 10-3/4 oz. cans cream of
    potato soup

2 c. sour cream
2 c. shredded Cheddar
    cheese, divided
2 c. cooked ham, cubed

Combine hashbrowns, soup, sour cream, 1-1/2 cups cheese and ham in a large mixing bowl. Pour into a greased 13"x9" baking pan. Top with remaining cheese. Bake at 350 degrees for 25 to 30 minutes. Serves 8 to 10.

Sharing a casserole with a friend who's feeling under the weather? Take along an old-fashioned water bottle, too...it'll be just right for keeping her warm & cozy.

Calico Bean Casserole

Linda Prosser
Seneca Falls, NY

This casserole is the best! You'll take it to potlucks, picnics or reunions and get rave reviews.

1 lb. ground beef or
   turkey, browned
1 lb. bacon, crisply cooked
   and crumbled
16-oz. can butter beans
15-1/2 oz. can kidney beans
17-oz. can lima beans

16-oz. can pork & beans
15-1/2 oz. can cannellini beans
1/2 c. brown sugar, packed
1 c. catsup
2 T. vinegar
salt and pepper to taste

Mix together all ingredients; pour in a lightly greased 13"x9" baking pan. Bake at 350 degrees for one hour. Serves 6 to 8.

6-Layer Country Casserole

Megan Hutchinson
Wisconsin Rapids, WI

The best thing is the ingredients are probably already in your kitchen.

3 potatoes, sliced
2 stalks celery, chopped
1 lb. ground beef, browned
1 onion, chopped

14-1/2 oz. can diced tomatoes
1 green pepper, sliced
Garnish: bread crumbs

Layer all ingredients, in order, in a lightly greased 13"x9" baking pan. Cover and bake at 325 degrees for one hour. Sprinkle with bread crumbs; return to oven for 5 to 10 minutes until golden. Serves 6 to 8.

Chicken & Corn Stuffing Bake

Debbie Haag
Almond, WI

A sweet cranberry glaze dresses this up enough for Sunday dinner.

1-3/4 c. cornbread stuffing mix
10-3/4 oz. can cream of
   chicken soup
1/2 c. corn
1 onion, finely chopped
1 T. butter

1/4 c. celery, chopped
4 boneless, skinless
   chicken breasts
1-1/2 T. cranberry-honey
   mustard

Combine stuffing mix, soup and corn in a large mixing bowl. Sauté onion in butter until tender; add to stuffing mix. Stir in celery. Pour into a greased 2-quart baking dish. Arrange chicken over stuffing; brush cranberry-honey mustard over top. Bake at 400 degrees for 30 to 40 minutes or until chicken juices run clear. Serves 4.

Home, the spot of earth supremely blest. A dearer, sweeter spot than all the rest.
-Robert Montgomery

Fiesta Casserole

Betty Martin
Lakeside, CA

A terrific overnight casserole that's loaded with flavor.

6 c. whole-wheat bread, cubed
4-1/2 oz. can chopped green
  chilies
16-oz. can corn, drained
4-oz. can black olives, drained
  and chopped

1 c. shredded mozzarella cheese
1 c. shredded Cheddar cheese
4 eggs, beaten
2 c. milk
1/8 t. pepper

Toss together bread and chilies; place in the bottom of a buttered
11"x7" baking pan. Arrange corn and olives over bread layer. Sprinkle
cheeses over top. Combine eggs, milk and pepper in a mixing bowl;
pour evenly over casserole. Cover with plastic wrap; refrigerate
4 hours or overnight. Uncover casserole and let stand at room
temperature while heating oven to 375 degrees. Bake for 35 to
45 minutes or until puffed and golden. Let stand 10 minutes before
cutting. Serves 6.

Share silly memories at the next family get-together. Ask everyone to jot down their favorites and toss them in a hat. Pull them out one at a time to read out loud...guaranteed giggles!

Savory Southern Casserole

Paula Eggleston
Knoxville, TN

In the South, grits are eaten with any meal of the day but this cheesy dish is great for a family cookout or barbecue.

4 c. water
1 onion, chopped
1 t. salt
1 c. quick-cooking grits, uncooked
3/4 c. butter, divided

1-1/2 lbs. pasteurized process cheese spread, cubed
garlic powder to taste
4 eggs
milk
2 c. corn flake cereal

Bring water, onion and salt to a boil; add grits. Remove from heat; stir to keep smooth. In a separate saucepan, melt 1/2 cup butter, cheese and garlic powder. In a small bowl, beat eggs with enough milk to make one cup; add to cheese mixture. Stir cheese mixture into grit mixture; pour into a greased 13"x9" baking pan. Melt remaining butter; stir in cereal. Sprinkle on top of grits. Bake at 350 degrees for 30 minutes. Serves 8 to 10.

Even though an old sprinkling can may have a hole in the bottom, don't toss it...what a nifty one-of-a-kind weather vane for a garden shed!

Broccoli-Cheddar Casserole

Lisa Gillette-Martin
San Jose, CA

This savory casserole is one you'll want to serve often...it goes with almost anything and couldn't be easier to make.

2 10-oz. pkgs. frozen chopped
   broccoli, thawed
2 eggs
1 onion, chopped
10-3/4 oz. can cream of
   celery soup

1 c. mayonnaise
1-1/2 c. shredded Cheddar
   cheese
1 c. bread crumbs

Combine all ingredients, except bread crumbs, in a large mixing bowl; pour into a buttered 2-quart baking dish. Sprinkle bread crumbs over top. Bake at 350 degrees for 30 minutes or until bubbly. Serves 4 to 6.

A Jack Frost Feast is a great idea for a chilly Autumn evening. Invite neighbors to bring a dish to share, get a big bonfire going and set out some plump pumpkins. Enjoy!

Beef & Mushroom Dish

Blanche Crago
Ostrander, OH

This August we'll celebrate our 70th wedding anniversary and this recipe was in the very first cookbook I had when we married!

2 T. shortening
2 lbs. round steak, cubed
1 onion, chopped
1 clove garlic, chopped
2 T. all-purpose flour
1 c. sour cream

4-oz. can sliced mushrooms
1/2 c. celery, chopped
8-oz. can tomato sauce
1 t. salt
1 T. Worcestershire sauce

Melt shortening in a large skillet. Add steak and cook over medium-high until browned. Remove steak; add onion and garlic to sauté in drippings. Reduce heat to low; blend in flour and sour cream, stirring constantly until thickened. Return steak to mixture and add remaining ingredients. Pour mixture into a greased 3-quart baking dish; bake at 350 degrees for 1-1/2 hours. Serves 6 to 8.

Look at flea market finds in a new way...a less-than-perfect desk can become a potting bench or a set of shutters can be hinged together to make a clever room divider.

Baked Spaghetti Casserole

Brenda Jahnke
Hastings, NE

*Take this to any get-together and you won't be
coming home with leftovers!*

1-1/2 lbs. ground beef
1 onion, chopped
salt and pepper to taste
1 t. chili powder
10-3/4 oz. can tomato soup
10-3/4 oz. can cream of
    mushroom soup

water
16-oz. pkg. spaghetti, cooked
1/3 c. catsup
1 c. shredded Cheddar cheese

Brown ground beef and onion; drain. Add salt, pepper, chili powder,
tomato soup, cream of mushroom soup and one soup can of water;
simmer 30 minutes. Place cooked spaghetti in an ungreased
13"x9" baking pan; top with beef mixture, stirring to combine. Spread
catsup over top and sprinkle with cheese. Bake at 350 degrees for
20 to 30 minutes until bubbly. Serves 6 to 8.

*Vintage tin pails are
ideal for grab & go
goodies...crayons
and markers for a
visit to grandma's or
seed packets and
tools for a trip
to the garden.*

Old-fashioned Sweets

Lemon Delight

Caroline Capper
Circleville, OH

Mama heard this recipe on the radio when I was a little girl in the 1940's. It's still one of our family's favorites.

2 eggs, separated
2 T. butter
3/4 c. sugar
2 T. all-purpose flour

1/4 c. lemon juice
1 c. milk
Optional: frozen whipped
   topping, thawed

Beat egg yolks in a small bowl; set aside. In a separate bowl, beat egg whites until stiff peaks form; set aside. In a medium-size mixing bowl, cream butter and sugar together; add flour and continue to cream mixture. Beat in egg yolks, lemon juice and milk; fold in egg whites. Pour mixture into an ungreased 12"x8" baking pan or individual custard cups. Bake at 360 degrees for 35 minutes. Top with whipped topping, if desired. Serves 4 to 6.

A photo charm bracelet will keep Mom's little sweeties near & dear. Old-fashioned ones can be found at tag sales or create your own by attaching tiny photo frames to a bracelet.

Sweet Gingers

*Joyce Davis
Greeley, CO*

*While they're baking, these cookies fill the house with a warm,
spicy aroma that's irresistible.*

3/4 c. shortening
1 c. sugar
1/4 c. molasses
1 egg
2 c. all-purpose flour

1/4 t. salt
1 t. baking soda
1 t. ground cloves
1 t. ground ginger

Cream together shortening, sugar and molasses. Add egg, mixing well.
Blend in remaining ingredients. Roll dough into walnut-size balls;
place on ungreased baking sheets and flatten slightly. Bake at 350 for
10 to 12 minutes. Makes 2 dozen.

Toffee

*Wendy Lee Paffenroth
Pine Island, NY*

What a treat...great for munching!

1 c. chopped walnuts
1/2 c. butter
3/4 c. brown sugar, packed

1/2 c. semi-sweet chocolate
chips

Butter an 8"x8" pan; spread walnuts on the bottom. In a saucepan,
heat butter and sugar; bring to a boil, stirring constantly. Cook until
mixture darkens, about 7 minutes; immediately pour over walnuts.
Sprinkle chocolate chips over top; cover with a baking sheet to hold in
heat until chocolate begins to melt. Spread chips over top; cut into
1-1/2 inch squares. Refrigerate; break into squares when cool. Makes
about one pound.

Granny's Fudge

Lee Ganey
Englewood, CO

Old-fashioned fudge...smooth and chocolatey.

4-1/2 c. sugar
5-oz. can evaporated milk
3 6-oz. pkgs. chocolate chips

1 c. butter, melted
Optional: 1 c. chopped nuts
1 t. vanilla extract

In a large saucepan, bring sugar and milk to a boil; continue cooking for 7 minutes. Stir in remaining ingredients, except vanilla. Remove from heat and stir in vanilla. Spread mixture into a greased 8"x8" pan; let cool. Makes about one pound.

Peanut Butter Fudge

Cheryl Bigony
Piqua, OH

We're hooked on on this recipe for creamy fudge!

3 c. sugar
3/4 c. margarine
2/3 c. evaporated milk
18-oz. jar creamy peanut butter

13-oz. jar marshmallow creme
1 c. crushed nuts
1 t. vanilla extract

Bring sugar, margarine and milk to a boil in a saucepan; boil 5 minutes, stirring constantly. Place peanut butter and marshmallow creme in a large bowl; pour sugar mixture over top, mixing well. Stir in nuts and vanilla. Quickly pour mixture into an ungreased 13"x9" pan; chill until set. Cut into squares. Makes 3 pounds.

Golden Bread Pudding

Betty Bullock
Denton, MD

Dusted with cinnamon-sugar, this sweet comfort food is like no other.

3 c. white bread, cubed
3 eggs, beaten
3 c. warm water
14-oz. can sweetened
　condensed milk

2 T. margarine, melted
1 T. vanilla extract
1/2 t. salt
Garnish: cinnamon-sugar

Place bread cubes in a buttered 9"x9" baking pan; set aside. In a large mixing bowl, combine all remaining ingredients; pour evenly over bread. Sprinkle with cinnamon-sugar. Bake at 350 degrees for 45 to 50 minutes. Serves 4 to 6.

Here's a keepsake that Grandma will cherish. Preserve the patter of little feet with a kids' stepping stone kit. Found at craft stores, all that's needed is water and little ones to press their feet (or hands!) into the mix...so sweet!

Peach-Walnut Crisp

Debbie Zlupko
Aston, PA

Serve this warm with a big scoop of vanilla ice cream...heavenly!

5 c. fresh or frozen peach slices,
    thawed
1 T. all-purpose flour
3 T. sugar
1/2 c. quick-cooking oats,
    uncooked

1/4 c. whole-wheat flour
2 T. wheat and barley cereal
1/2 c. brown sugar, packed
1/4 t. nutmeg
2 T. chopped walnuts
1/4 c. buttermilk

Drain and discard any juice from peaches; arrange slices in an ungreased 8" round baking pan. In a small bowl, stir together all-purpose flour and sugar. Sprinkle over peaches, tossing to coat. In a separate bowl, combine remaining ingredients, except buttermilk; mix well. Pour buttermilk over oat mixture and combine mixture with a fork until it resembles coarse crumbs. Sprinkle oat mixture on top of peaches. Bake at 350 degrees for 30 to 35 minutes or until top is golden. Serves 6.

Make family pictures extra special. Choose a frame, 14"x16", and have a white mat cut with a 5"x7" opening in the center. Slip in a picture, then cover the mat with anything that brings back fond memories...ticket stubs, post cards or kids' artwork!

Cinnamon Cake

L. Santa Ana
Lomita, CA

Inside each slice you'll find sweet swirls of cinnamon.

18-1/4 oz. pkg. yellow cake mix
3.4-oz. pkg. instant vanilla
   pudding mix
3/4 c. oil
3/4 c. water

1 t. vanilla extract
1/2 t. butter flavoring
4 eggs
1/4 c. sugar
1-1/4 t. cinnamon

Combine first 6 ingredients in a large mixing bowl. Beat in eggs, one at a time, until mixture is smooth; set aside. In a separate bowl, combine sugar and cinnamon. Grease a Bundt® pan and sprinkle with half the cinnamon-sugar mixture. Pour half the cake batter in pan; sprinkle remaining cinnamon-sugar mix on top. Pour remaining batter on top. Bake at 350 degrees for one hour or until golden. Allow cake to cool for several minutes before removing from pan; pour icing over top while still warm. Serves 10 to 12.

Icing:

1 c. powdered sugar
3 T. milk

1/4 t. butter flavoring

Mix all ingredients until smooth.

For some terrific
summertime memories,
set up an old-fashioned
lemonade stand with the kids!

Peanut Butter Bars

Cindy Stauring
Hatfield, PA

*The kids will love these...chocolate sandwiched
between layers of peanut butter.*

1/2 c. butter, softened
1/2 c. brown sugar, packed
1/2 c. sugar
1 egg
1/3 c. creamy peanut butter
1/2 t. vanilla extract

1/2 t. baking soda
1/4 t. salt
1 c. all-purpose flour
1 c. quick-cooking oats,
  uncooked
1 c. semi-sweet chocolate chips

Cream together butter and sugars; blend in egg. Add peanut butter and vanilla. In a separate bowl, combine baking soda, salt, flour and oats; gradually add to creamed mixture. Spread batter into a greased 13"x9" baking pan. Bake at 350 degrees for 20 to 25 minutes or until lightly golden. Immediately sprinkle with chocolate chips; let stand for 5 minutes. Spread melted chips then drizzle with glaze; swirl with a knife. Let cool; cut into thin slices. Makes about 2 dozen.

Glaze:

1/2 c. powdered sugar
1/4 c. creamy peanut butter

2 to 4 T. milk

Mix together all ingredients.

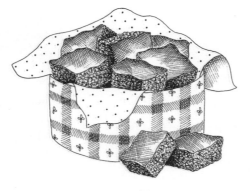

Soft Sugar Cookies

*Dayna Hale
Galena, OH*

Oh-so soft...just what a sugar cookie should be.

1 c. shortening	1 t. baking soda
2 c. sugar	1 t. salt
2 eggs	4 c. all-purpose flour
2 t. vanilla extract	1 c. milk
2 t. baking powder	powdered sugar

Cream shortening and sugar. Add eggs and vanilla; set aside. In a separate bowl, combine baking powder, baking soda, salt and flour; add to creamed mixture alternately with milk, beating well. Chill dough one to 2 hours. Drop by teaspoonfuls into powdered sugar and roll into balls. Place on greased baking sheets. Bake at 350 degrees for 8 to 10 minutes. Makes 4 to 5 dozen.

Glass apothecary jars are big and roomy which makes them ideal for holding a growing collection of cookie cutters!

Grandma Merle's Apple Cake

Carol Dean
Chico, CA

*My dear mother-in-law passed this famous recipe on to me.
She made in every year at Christmas, so it's been my
husband's favorite dessert since he was a little boy.*

1 c. brown sugar, packed
1 c. sugar
2 c. all-purpose flour
2 t. baking soda
2 t. cinnamon
1 t. salt

3/4 c. chopped nuts
3 eggs
1/2 c. milk
2 t. vanilla extract
4 to 5 apples, cored, peeled
    and diced

Mix together all ingredients, one at a time, in the order listed. Pour into a greased 13"x9" baking pan. Bake at 350 degrees for 40 to 45 minutes. Cool on wire rack before icing. Serves 10 to 12.

Icing:

4 T. butter
8-oz. pkg. cream cheese
2 c. powdered sugar

2 t. vanilla extract
1/8 t. salt

Blend together all ingredients until smooth.

*For someone far away, a care package of sweets is a
terrific surprise! Along with baked goodies, tuck in
a phone card and some family photos.*

Vanilla Drop Cookies

Susan Biffignani
Fenton, MO

*This recipe has been handed down to 3 generations from
my great-grandmother. I've already added it to a special book
for my daughter who is only 6 years old.*

3/4 c. butter
1-1/4 c. sugar
2 eggs, beaten
1 t. vanilla extract

3 c. all-purpose flour
3 t. baking powder
3/4 t. salt
2/3 c. milk

Cream butter and add sugar; beat until light. Beat in eggs; add vanilla.
In a separate bowl, sift together flour, baking powder and salt; stir in
milk. Add flour mixture to creamed mixture; blend well. Chill dough
for 3 to 4 hours. Drop by teaspoonfuls onto ungreased baking sheets.
Bake at 350 degrees for 6 minutes or until lightly golden. Makes
2 to 3 dozen.

*If there's a bake sale coming up, try this: offer a
sampler plate for those who just can't decide. Fill it
with 3 or 4 different cookies, fudge
and a slice of cake!*

Grandma Knotts' Tapioca

Brooke & Brittany Knotts
Cable, OH

We especially love Grandma's tapioca on a chilly Autumn day with warm chocolate chip cookies served alongside...yum!

4 c. milk	3 eggs, separated
1/8 t. salt	3/4 c. sugar, divided
4-1/2 T. pearled tapioca	1-1/2 t. vanilla extract

Combine milk, salt and tapioca in a saucepan. Cook over low heat, stirring often; bring to a boil. In a separate bowl, beat egg whites with 1/2 cup sugar until stiff peaks form; set aside. In a separate bowl, beat egg yolks with remaining sugar; add to boiling tapioca mixture. Bring to a boil, then remove from heat. Stir in egg white mixture; let stand 15 minutes and stir in vanilla. Serves 4 to 6.

Sugar Cookies
2 cups flour
1 cup sugar
1/2 cup butter
2 Large eggs

Put out the welcome mat and invite friends over for dessert...keep it simple so everyone's free to visit.

Chocolate-Peanut Butter Squares

Vicki Exum
Roanoke Rapids, NC

Tastes just like the famous candy!

2-1/2 c. powdered sugar
1/2 c. brown sugar, packed
1 t. vanilla extract
2 c. creamy peanut butter

1/2 c. plus 4 T. margarine,
  divided
6-oz. pkg. semi-sweet
  chocolate chips

Combine sugars, vanilla, peanut butter and 1/2 cup margarine; press into an ungreased 13"x9" baking pan. Melt together remaining margarine and chocolate; pour over peanut butter mixture and refrigerate until firm. Cut into squares. Makes 2 dozen.

Graham Cracker Brownies

Peggy Duzik
Sioux City, IA

Substitute mint chocolate chips for a whole new taste.

2 c. graham cracker crumbs
1 c. semi-sweet chocolate chips
1 t. baking powder

1/8 t. salt
14-oz. can sweetened
  condensed milk

Combine all ingredients in a medium mixing bowl. Spread into a greased 8"x8" baking pan. Bake at 350 degrees for 30 to 35 minutes or until a toothpick inserted near the center comes out clean. Cool on a wire rack and cut into squares. Makes 1-1/2 dozen.

What good fortune to grow up in a home where there are grandparents.

-Suzanne Lafollette

Lemon Meringue Pie

Marilyn Williams
Westerville, OH

So often I would come home from school and Mom would have made this pie...it would be cooling on the counter and I could barely wait to have a bite. Now I make it for my girls and they love it too!

14-oz. can sweetened
    condensed milk
1/2 c. lemon juice

3 eggs, separated
9-inch graham cracker pie crust
15 to 20 vanilla wafers

Whisk together milk and lemon juice in a large mixing bowl; blend in egg yolks, reserving egg whites for meringue. Pour mixture into pie crust and cover with meringue. Line edge of pie with vanilla wafers, sticking each halfway into pie. Bake at 325 degrees for 10 to 15 minutes or until top is golden. Serves 6 to 8.

Meringue:

3 egg whites
1/4 t. cream of tartar

1/4 c. to 1/2 c. sugar

Beat together egg whites and cream of tartar until stiff peaks form; add sugar to desired consistency and taste.

Spreading meringue so it touches the edges of the pie crust is the secret to keeping it from shrinking...works every time!

Old South Pound Cake

Delinda Blakney
Bridgeview, IL

If you thought the days were gone when pound cake really
did take a pound of each ingredient...you were wrong!

1 lb. butter
1 lb. sugar
10 eggs, separated
1 lb. all-purpose flour

1/2 t. salt
1 t. lemon flavoring or vanilla
   extract

Cream butter; add sugar and beat well. In a separate bowl, beat egg
yolks; add to creamed mixture. Combine flour and salt; stir into
creamed mixture. Add lemon flavoring or vanilla. Beat egg whites
until stiff peaks form; fold into cake batter. Pour into a greased Bundt®
pan. Bake at 300 degrees for 1-1/2 hours. Makes 10 to 12 servings.

Homemade whipped cream is so easy!
Combine one cup heavy cream with 1/4 cup
powdered sugar and one teaspoon vanilla extract in
a chilled bowl. Beat until stiff peaks form and
dollop on a big slice of cake or pie!

Triple-Layer Dessert

Megan Shutt
Damascus, MD

This has been my favorite dessert for as long as I can remember. My aunt shared it with my mother after she and my father married, and my mother passed it to me after I was married. I can't wait to give it to my daughter, now one year old, and continue the tradition.

1-1/2 c. all-purpose flour
1 c. chopped nuts
3/4 c. butter, softened
8-oz. pkg. plus 3-oz. pkg. cream
    cheese, softened
1-1/2 c. powdered sugar
8-oz. container frozen whipped
    topping, thawed and divided

3.4-oz. pkg. instant vanilla
    pudding mix
3.9-oz. pkg. instant chocolate
    pudding mix
2 c. milk
Garnish: semi-sweet
    chocolate, grated

Blend together flour, nuts and butter; pat into an ungreased 13"x9" glass baking dish. Bake at 350 degrees for 25 minutes; cool completely. In medium bowl, beat cream cheese and powdered sugar together until smooth; fold in one cup whipped topping. Spread over crust. In a separate bowl, combine vanilla and chocolate pudding mixes; stir in milk and spread over cream cheese layer. Spread remaining whipped topping over pudding layer; sprinkle grated chocolate on top. Chill overnight. Serves 6 to 8.

Mom's Chocolate Eclairs

Amber Brandt
Tucson, AZ

When my brother and I were young, these were one of my mother's extra-special treats that we always looked forward to and enjoyed.

4.6-oz. pkg. cook and serve
   vanilla pudding mix
1 c. water

1/2 c. butter
1 c. all-purpose flour
4 eggs

Cook pudding according to package directions. Pour into a bowl; place plastic wrap directly on the surface and refrigerate until chilled. In a 2-quart saucepan, heat water and butter to a rolling boil; whisk in flour. Mix well over low heat about one minute or until mixture forms a ball; remove from heat. Beat in all eggs until smooth. Butter hands and shape dough into twelve, 4-1/2"x1-1/2" rectangles; place on an ungreased baking sheet. Bake at 400 degrees for 35 to 40 minutes or until puffed and golden. Do not open oven during baking. Allow pastries to cool away from any draft. Slice each rectangle on 3 sides; pull out and discard gooey dough inside. Remove chilled pudding and stir; fill each eclair with pudding. Spread icing on top and refrigerate until serving. Makes 12.

Icing:

1-oz. sq. unsweetened baking
   chocolate
1 t. butter

1 c. powdered sugar
2 to 3 T. hot water

Melt chocolate and butter together over low heat in a small saucepan. Remove from heat. Stir in powdered sugar and 2 tablespoons hot water until smooth; add up to one additional tablespoon if necessary.

Grandma Ruth's Molasses Cookies

Audrey Bretz
Ripley, NY

When I asked my grandma for this recipe, she told me that she never measured the ingredients! We worked together to come up with approximate measurements and developed this recipe.

1/2 c. margarine, softened
1 c. brown sugar, packed
1 egg
1/4 c. molasses
1 t. salt

1 t. baking soda
1/2 t. cinnamon
1/2 t. ground cloves
2-1/2 c. all-purpose flour

Cream together margarine, sugar, egg and molasses. Mix in remaining ingredients to form a stiff dough. Drop by teaspoonfuls onto greased baking sheets; press each cookie to 1/4-inch thickness using the bottom of a drinking glass dipped in sugar. Bake at 350 degrees for 8 to 10 minutes. Makes 3-1/2 dozen.

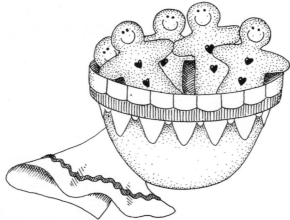

At the next flea market, look for small beaded baskets or Christmas ornaments...a sparkly 1950's fad that's still fun today!

Fresh Blueberry Pie

Jo Ann

Use a tiny cookie cutter for cut-outs to decorate the top crust.

3/4 c. sugar
3 T. cornstarch
1/8 t. salt
1/2 t. cinnamon

4 c. blueberries
2 9-inch pie crusts
1 T. lemon juice
2 T. butter

Combine sugar, cornstarch, salt and cinnamon in a small bowl; sprinkle over blueberries. Line a 9" pie plate with one crust; pour berry mixture inside. Sprinkle with lemon juice and dot with butter. Roll out remaining pie crust to fit the top; crimp and flute edges. Vent top. Bake at 425 degrees for 40 to 50 minutes or until crust is golden. Serves 6 to 8.

Family Easter egg hunts almost always mean lots of sweets, but why not fill plastic eggs with bracelets & beads, rubber stamps, charms or puzzle pieces...just for fun!

Grandma's Peanut Butter Pie

Kristina Wyatt
Madera, CA

My grandma is a wonderful cook and baker and my family often jokes that she could make an entire meal out of flour and water! When we would visit, she always had a fresh-baked pie waiting.

1/2 c. boiling water
4 T. cornstarch, divided
3/4 c. powdered sugar
1/2 c. creamy peanut butter
3/4 c. sugar, divided
1 T. all-purpose flour
1/8 t. salt

3 eggs
3 c. milk
2 t. butter
2 t. vanilla extract
1/4 t. cream of tartar
9-inch deep-dish pie crust,
    prebaked

In a small saucepan, mix together boiling water and one tablespoon cornstarch. Cook and stir constantly until clear and thick; set aside to cool. In a small bowl, combine powdered sugar and peanut butter to resemble coarse crumbs; set aside. In a 2-quart saucepan, stir together 1/2 cup sugar, remaining cornstarch, flour and salt. Separate eggs, placing whites in a separate bowl; set aside to warm to room temperature. Add egg yolks and milk to sugar mixture; whisk until combined. Bring mixture to a boil over medium heat; cook and stir for 2 minutes. Remove from heat and stir in butter and vanilla. Sprinkle 1/3 peanut butter mixture over pie crust bottom; layer half batter over crumbs. Sprinkle another 1/3 peanut butter mix over batter and top with remaining batter; set aside. Add cornstarch mixture and cream of tartar to egg whites; beat until soft peaks form. Gradually sprinkle remaining sugar over mix until stiff peaks form. Spread meringue over pie, being sure to touch edges of crust to seal. Sprinkle remaining 1/3 peanut butter crumbs around top edge of pie. Bake at 375 degrees for 8 to 10 minutes or until meringue is golden. Cool completely before serving. Serves 6 to 8.

Give a family cookbook or vacation album an extra-special cover...secure a lightweight picture frame on the front and slip in a favorite photo.

Peaches & Cream Cheesecake

Betty Rowland
Hillsboro, OH

This will disappear like magic!

3/4 c. all-purpose flour
1/2 t. salt
1/2 c. milk
1 egg
1 t. baking powder
3.4-oz. pkg. instant vanilla
   pudding mix

3 T. butter
15-oz. can sliced peaches, juice
   reserved
8-oz. pkg. cream cheese,
   softened
1/2 c. plus 1 T. sugar, divided
1 t. cinnamon

Blend together flour, salt, milk, egg, baking powder, pudding mix and butter; beat for 2 minutes. Pour into a greased 9" round pan; arrange peaches on top. In a separate bowl, mix cream cheese, 3 tablespoons of reserved juice and 1/2 cup sugar; beat for 2 minutes. Spoon over peaches. Combine remaining sugar and cinnamon; sprinkle on top. Bake at 350 degrees for 30 to 35 minutes. Serves 6 to 8.

Display old photos in a new way. Look for 2 clear drinking glasses, one needs to be slightly smaller in diameter than the other. Place the smaller glass inside the larger one and then slip photos in the open space between...very clever!

Old-Fashioned Rice Pudding

Linda Hensz
Milanville, PA

Passed down from our Canadian grandmother, this is always a treat.

1 c. prepared brown rice
1 egg
1-1/2 c. milk
1/2 c. whipping cream

1 T. honey
1/2 c. raisins
1 T. butter
cinnamon to taste

Place rice in an ungreased 1-1/2 quart baking dish; set aside. Beat egg lightly with milk and cream in a small mixing bowl; pour over rice. Stir in honey and raisins. Dot top with butter and sprinkle with cinnamon. Bake at 275 degrees for 1-1/2 hours. Makes about 4 servings.

A family cookbook is a really wonderful way to preserve all the tried & true favorite recipes. Send letters, e-mails or give everyone a call so they can add their best-loved recipes. Share copies at the next get-together for a gift that will be treasured.

Mom's Strawberry Angel Food Roll

Wendy Bostic
Kimper, KY

So beautiful sliced and unbeatable topped with real whipped cream.

14-1/2 oz. pkg. angel food
   cake mix
1 qt. strawberries, hulled
   and sliced

1/4 c. sugar
2 c. whipping cream
3 T. powdered sugar

Prepare cake according to package directions; pour into an greased jelly roll pan lined with wax paper. Bake at 375 degrees for 10 to 12 minutes. Turn cake onto a towel dusted with powdered sugar. Peel off wax paper. Starting at narrow end, roll up cake and towel together; cool on wire rack for 20 minutes, seam-side down. In a mixing bowl, combine strawberries and sugar; set aside. In a separate bowl, beat cream until foamy. Add powdered sugar; continue beating until soft peaks form. Drain any liquid from berries. Unroll cake and remove from towel. Spread cake with half whipped cream mixture; top with strawberries. Re-roll cake; place on a plate seam-side down. Serve with remaining whipped cream. Serves 10 to 12.

Start a new tradition...each time a new baby arrives in the family plant a tree. It's amazing to see how they both grow!

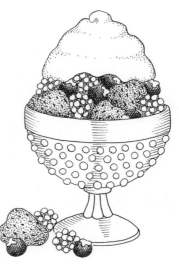

Holiday Fruit Cake

Peggy Wasley
Vestal, NY

I can remember both my grandmother and mother baking this cake...the kitchen would smell so nice!

2 c. hot water
1 c. shortening
2 t. cinnamon
2 c. sugar
2 c. raisins
2 t. ground cloves
1 t. salt

4 c. all-purpose flour
1 c. chopped nuts
2 t. vanilla extract
2 t. baking soda
14-1/2 oz. jar maraschino
    cherries, drained and sliced

Combine first 6 ingredients in a large saucepan and bring to a boil; remove from heat and allow to cool. Mix in remaining ingredients; pour into two, 9"x5" loaf pans. Bake at 350 degrees for one hour. Makes 2 loaves.

Spend family night playing some old-fashioned games...charades is one that will have everyone laughing!

Grandma's Chocolate Drop Cookies

Sue Reynolds
Saint Louis, MO

*As a kid, my husband would often stay with his grandma & grandpa
to help on their farm. They would make homemade ice cream
and these cookies...his favorites.*

2 c. sugar
1/4 c. baking cocoa
1/2 c. milk
1/4 c. butter
1/2 c. creamy peanut butter

1 t. vanilla extract
3 c. quick-cooking oats,
  uncooked
Optional: 1/2 c. chopped nuts

Mix together sugar, cocoa, milk and butter in a saucepan; bring to a
boil and boil for one minute. Remove from heat; stir in remaining
ingredients. Drop by teaspoonfuls onto wax paper and allow to cool.
Makes 2 to 3 dozen.

*Old metal picnic
baskets are just the
right size for keeping
coloring books &
crayons together and
the folding handles
mean they can be
toted anywhere!*

Apple Pie Wedges

Catherine Gray
Jacksonville, FL

Sweetly spiced apple butter in a tender crust...served with icy milk, it's one of the best things in the world.

1 c. butter	2-1/3 c. all-purpose flour
2/3 c. sugar	1 t. cinnamon
1 egg yolk	1/2 t. apple pie spice
1/3 c. apple butter	1/2 t. vanilla extract

Beat butter and sugar together; beat in egg yolk and apple butter. Add remaining ingredients; beat until well blended. Divide dough in half; shape each half into a 6-inch circle on wax paper. Refrigerate for 30 minutes. Press each circle into separate 9" pie plates covering plates completely; flute edges with a wooden spoon. Score each pie into 8 wedges, using fork tines. Bake both at 350 degrees for 35 minutes; place on a wire rack to cool. Cut into wedges. Makes 16.

A collection of patterned handkerchiefs can be turned into a one-of-a-kind bedspread in an afternoon! It's easy...just stitch the hankies together and layer with quilt batting and a sheet.

German Butter Cookies

Norma Maiwald
Lohrville, IA

You can buy butter cookies at the grocery store,
but homemade is still best.

1 c. plus 1 T. unsalted butter
1-1/3 c. sugar
1 t. vanilla extract

1 egg
3 c. all-purpose flour
1 t. baking powder

Melt butter in a saucepan, stirring constantly until golden. Pour butter
into a mixing bowl; add sugar, vanilla and egg. Whip for 20 minutes
until mixture turns nearly white in color. In a separate bowl, sift
together flour and baking powder; gradually add to whipped mixture.
Turn dough onto a flat surface; knead several times. Divide dough in
half; form each half into two, 12-inch rolls. Chill rolls one hour; cut
into 3/8-inch cookie slices. Place slices on ungreased baking sheets;
bake at 325 degrees for 16 minutes. Makes about 3 dozen.

For a chocolatey treat, dip half of each
German Butter Cookie in melted chocolate...yum!

Chocolate Chip Cookies

Becky Rowland
Belpre, OH

No cookie jar is complete without this all-time favorite!

2-1/3 c. all-purpose flour
1 t. baking soda
1 c. margarine, softened
1/4 c. sugar
3/4 c. brown sugar, packed
1 t. vanilla extract

5-1/4 oz. pkg. instant vanilla
    pudding mix
2 eggs
12-oz. pkg. semi-sweet
    chocolate chips

Mix together flour, baking soda, margarine, sugars, vanilla and pudding mix; beat until smooth and creamy. Beat in eggs. Stir in chocolate chips. Drop by teaspoonfuls onto ungreased baking sheets. Bake at 375 degrees for 8 to 10 minutes or until golden. Makes 2 to 3 dozen.

A big chalkboard in the kitchen is handy spot to keep a running grocery list.

Carrot Cake

Teri Williams
Sistersville, WV

Whether it's for a cake auction, bake sale, birthday or if you just have a sweet tooth, this classic with cream cheese icing is always a hit.

1 c. oil
1 t. vanilla extract
4 eggs
1 t. salt
2 t. cinnamon
2 c. sugar

2 c. all-purpose flour
2 t. baking soda
2 t. baking powder
1 c. chopped walnuts
3 c. carrots, grated

Mix together oil, vanilla and eggs in a small bowl; set aside. In a large bowl, combine salt, cinnamon, sugar, flour, baking soda and baking powder; stir in egg mixture. Add nuts and carrots, mixing well. Pour batter into 3, greased and floured 8" round cake pans. Bake layers at 350 degrees for 35 minutes or until inserted toothpick comes out clean. Cool in pans for several minutes, then invert onto wire racks to cool completely. Spread icing between layers and over top and sides of cake. Serves 8 to 10.

Icing:

1/2 c. butter
8-oz. pkg. cream cheese

2 c. powdered sugar

Beat together all ingredients until smooth.

Grandma's Molasses Popcorn Balls

Cindy Hertz
Hummelstown, PA

My grandmother made these with my mom, and my mom made them every Christmas with me as a child. The best part was when the baking soda and butter were added...Mom said it was magic.

4 qts. popped popcorn
1 c. molasses
4 T. sugar

1 t. baking soda
1 t. butter

Place popcorn in a large bowl; set aside. Bring molasses and sugar to a boil in a large saucepan; boil for 20 minutes until mixture reaches the soft-ball stage, or 234 to 243 degrees on a candy thermometer. Remove from heat and quickly stir in baking soda and butter. Pour mixture over popcorn, stirring to coat. Grease hands with butter; shape popcorn into apple-size balls. Wrap individually in plastic wrap. Makes one to 2 dozen.

Hang a tire swing...big and little kids will love it!

Grandma Gracie's Lemon Cake
Denise Grace Musgrave
Shelbyville, IN

An excellent cook for her 6 kids, 18 grandchildren and 35 great-grandchildren, this is one my grandmother's best recipes.

18-1/4 oz. pkg. yellow cake mix
3.4 oz. pkg. instant lemon
  pudding mix
3/4 c. oil
3/4 c. water
4 eggs

Mix together all ingredients. Pour into a greased 13"x9" baking pan. Bake at 350 degrees for 35 to 40 minutes or until toothpick inserted in center comes out clean. Remove cake from oven and immediately poke holes through the cake with a fork; pour glaze over top. Serves 10 to 12.

Glaze:

2 c. powdered sugar
2 T. butter, melted
2 T. water
1/3 c. lemon juice

Combine all ingredients.

You're never too old for a tea party! Make iced cookies, sugar-dusted cakes and fill dainty cups with soothing chamomile tea...a delightful way for Grandma to spend an afternoon with her granddaughters.

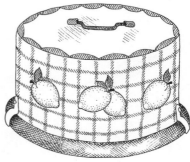

Iced Shortbread Cookies

Nancy Morris
Adams, TN

Buttery and rich...just like the perfect shortbread should be.

3 T. sugar   1/2 c. butter, softened
1-1/4 c. all-purpose flour

Stir together sugar and flour in a mixing bowl; cut in butter with a fork
or pastry cutter. Mix until a soft dough forms. Shape cookies into
walnut-size balls and place on ungreased baking sheets. Press thumb
in the center of each cookie. Bake at 325 degrees for 20 to 25 minutes
or until lightly golden; remove to cooling racks. Spread icing in the
center of each cookie. Makes one to 2 dozen.

Icing:

1/4 c. butter   Optional: food coloring
2 c. powdered sugar   milk
1 t. vanilla extract

Melt butter in a saucepan; cook over medium heat until butter is dark
golden in color. Combine butter and sugar in a mixing bowl; add
vanilla and food coloring if desired. Add milk, if needed, for spreading
consistency.

*Enjoy a girls' day
antique spree! Get
everyone together,
rent a truck and
have a ball!*

Butterscotch Dumplings

Heather Campbell
Orem, UT

This is a delicious old-fashioned family recipe. For a larger batch, triple the syrup ingredients and double the dumpling ingredients.

1/2 c. plus 1 T. sugar, divided
1/2 c. brown sugar, packed
3 T. butter, divided
1 c. water

1 c. all-purpose flour
1 t. baking powder
1/2 c. milk

Melt together 1/2 cup sugar, brown sugar, one tablespoon butter and water in a saucepan. Pour into a lightly greased 8"x8" glass baking dish. Mix remaining ingredients together, stirring just until combined; layer on top of syrup. Bake at 350 degrees for 23 to 27 minutes or until golden. Serves 5.

Be inspired by 1940's bridge tally cards when making placecards! Leave off the guests' names and use buttons, beads and felt scraps to resemble each person. Part of the fun is letting them guess which one is theirs!

Index

Breads

Breakfast

Desserts

Index

Main Dishes

Salads

Index

Sides

Soups

We've cooked up a whole collection of Gooseberry Patch® books!

Have a taste for more? Call us toll-free at

1-800-854-6673

We'll send you our latest catalog filled with snowmen, Santas, ornaments, candles, cookie cutters, gourmet goodies, calendars, giftwrap, pottery, collectibles and MORE...including our best-selling cookbooks!

Phone us:
1·800·854·6673

Fax us:
1·740·363·7225

Visit our website:
www.gooseberrypatch.com

Send us your favorite recipe!

Include the memory that makes it special for you too! If we select your recipe for a brand new **Gooseberry Patch** cookbook, your name will appear right along with it...and you'll receive a FREE copy of the book! Mail to:

Vickie & Jo Ann
Gooseberry Patch, Dept. Book
600 London Road
Delaware, Ohio 43015

*Please include the number of servings and all other necessary information!

223